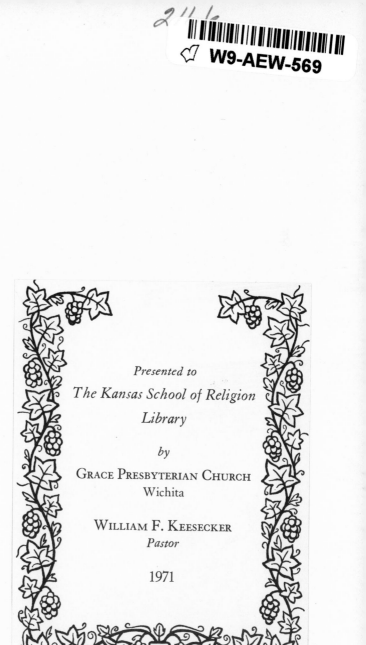

Secularization and the Protestant Prospect

BOOKS BY DAVID B. HARNED
PUBLISHED BY THE WESTMINSTER PRESS

The Ambiguity of Religion
Theology and the Arts

Secularization

and the

Protestant Prospect

Edited, with an introduction, by

James F. Childress

and

David B. Harned

THE WESTMINSTER PRESS
Philadelphia

STANDARD BOOK No. 664-24876-4

LIBRARY OF CONGRESS CATALOG CARD No. 77-98118

Seculaism

Published by The Westminster Press ®
Philadelphia, Pennsylvania

PRINTED IN THE UNITED STATES OF AMERICA

Contents

List of Contributors

Robert N. Bellah has taught at Harvard University and is presently Ford Professor of Sociology and Comparative Studies at the University of California, Berkeley. He is the author of *Tokugawa Religion* and editor of *Religion and Progress in Modern Asia*.

Julian N. Hartt, author of *A Christian Critique of American Culture* and *Theology and the Church in the University,* is Noah H. Porter Professor of Theology and Chairman of the Department of Religious Studies at Yale University.

Samuel Laeuchli teaches in the Department of Religion, Temple University. Among his various writings is *The Language of Faith: An Introduction to the Semantic Dilemma of the Early Church.*

David Little is Assistant Professor of Social Ethics at Yale Divinity School and author of *Religion, Order and Law* and *American Foreign Policy and Moral Rhetoric.*

Thomas Luckmann now teaches at Johann Wolfgang Goethe University in Frankfurt, Germany, and is the author of *The Invisible Religion* and a coauthor (with Peter Berger) of *The Social Construction of Reality.* Previously he taught at Hobart College and The New School for Social Research.

Talcott Parsons is Professor of Sociology at Harvard University. He is the author of several books, which include *The Structure of Social Action; The Social System; Structure and Process in Modern Societies;* and *Sociological Theory and Modern Society.*

Larry Shiner teaches in the Department of Religion, Cornell College, Mount Vernon, Iowa. He has studied secularization from several perspectives; in addition to articles on this subject, he has written *The Secularization of History,* a study of Gogarten.

Charles C. West, author of *Communism and the Theologians* and *Outside the Camp,* an examination of the church in mission, is Stephen Colwell Professor of Christian Ethics at Princeton Theological Seminary.

Preface

SECULARIZATION is and will remain a vital issue for Christian thought in the twentieth century. Theological interpretations of it, however, will gain new amplitude and relevance as theologians draw more fully upon sociological analysis and grow more familiar with the different sociological theories that shape such analysis. The church will err if its reflections upon secularization are fashioned by theological commitments that are not informed by sociological wisdom.

Robert Bellah and Thomas Luckmann describe two divergent ways in which religion continues to flourish within modern secularized society. In a very different vein, Talcott Parsons comments upon the institutionalization of Christian values outside the ecclesiastical establishment. The context for these essays is Larry Shiner's discussion of the numerous ways that the concept of secularization has been recently used in sociological research and, by implication, in theology as well.

Charles West stresses the historical relationship between the Biblical tradition and secularization. David Little contends that the autonomy of the individual as moral agent is an element within rather than a denial of the Christian heritage. Although Julian N. Hartt sees traditional questions of meaning and value as perennial and their ontological implications as inescapable, Samuel Laeuchli insists that Christians must find a new syntax and grammar if the gospel is to be faithfully proclaimed in our "age of secularization."

The editors wish to express their gratitude to Mrs. Doris S. Mays, secretary of the Department of Religious Studies at the University of Virginia, for services both considerable and unstintingly given.

I

Introduction—Secularization and Protestant Faith

It was the best of times, it was the worst of times, it was the age of wisdom, it was the age of foolishness, it was the epoch of belief, it was the epoch of incredulity, it was the season of Light, it was the season of Darkness, it was the spring of hope, it was the winter of despair, we had everything before us, we had nothing before us, we were all going direct to Heaven, we were all going direct the other way—in short, the period was so far like the present period, that some of its noisiest authorities insisted on its being received, for good or for evil, in the superlative degree of comparison only.[1]

Dickens' paragraph is a cautionary tale, for superlatives are no less idiomatic today than in the age of the French Revolution. Yet there are periods when the processes of time and the ambiguity of the times peculiarly conspire to enforce upon men a profound sense of mingled promise and loss, novelty and dislocation. *Secularization,* perhaps because it is so elusive of definition, has seemed an apt word to describe our world. But it is often more fashionable than descriptive. It is intended to designate what is happening in and to the church as well as in and to the world. Sometimes, however, its meaning is eroded by the obscurity of its real significance for religion. Sometimes, especially when it is used in a theological context, its significance is vitiated by the obscurity of its reference to our common life. Theologians not infrequently have employed secularization as a mere principium, have glimpsed only the surface of the revolutions in our time, and have been too quick to applaud or disapprove. Consequently, those who have been most attentive to the rhythms of social change have often become grudging in their use of the word.[2] Nevertheless, secularization has become a focus about which theologians could gather with those who speak in other tongues. Too often the tongues have been desperately confused, and from this Babel there is no exit except by way of serious and sustained attention to matters of definition. That, however, lies still with the future.

Secularization has entered the province of theology by many doors. Numerous writers believe they have spied a new man in our midst, a secular man who no longer shares the premises of *homo religiosus* and who requires a version of Christian faith that will be stripped of all its traditional religious dress. Others have understood secularization to mean a revolutionary complex of social processes that calls for a new view of the forms and mission of the church, as well as of its role in the relationship between the world and God. Still others have encountered the issue first of all as a phenomenon within the churches, blunting the edge of their witness and rendering them ever more difficult to distinguish from other social institutions.

Certainly the recent concern with secularization has afforded a new perspective upon the Bible. Many theologians argue that the roots of contemporary social change lie in Scripture itself. Even if there is no direct causal relationship in a historical sense, at least there seems to be Biblical warrant for the advocacy of secularization as congruent with Christian faith. For those who argue in this vein, secularization has tended to be synonymous with the historicizing of man's understanding of himself. It designates the transition from mythic patterns of thought that stress man's unity with the world to historical patterns that emphasize his responsibility for it. Other writers have employed the term "secularization" to designate the source of the constraint to hammer out a new grammar and rhetoric of faith that would reduce the gospel to its ethical dimension, in the belief that not only traditional metaphysical language but any notion of divine transcendence has been rendered anachronous by cultural and historical change. Still others have emphasized the distinction between religion and revelation, in order to insist that man is redeemed *sola gratia* and that religion offers him no privileged position before God. Therefore, it has scarcely been possible for them to regard secularization as an occasion for polemics against the godlessness of the world. So the word has come to be used in many ways and for many purposes in contemporary Christian thought, inviting considerable confusion in theology and even greater disarray in conversation with other disciplines. Nevertheless, the processes of social change offer no promise to abate their pace until we have put our semantic household in order.

The antecedents of contemporary theological concern with secularization do not lie in the attempts of the nineteenth century to reconcile Christianity and modern culture so much as they do in the work of Karl Barth. *The Epistle to the Romans* signified a new departure in Protestant thought because Barth did not champion *homo religiosus* but argued that Christians are "compelled to set the righteousness of faith over against all religious and ecclesiastical being and having and doing."[3] He insisted that the gospel is folly and scandal for religious man as much as for secular man, and for the Christian version of *homo religiosus* as much as for the Jewish or Greek version. Religion stands no less under the judgment of God than does any other form of cultural activity; if it is justified when it appears in Christian guise, it is justified *sola gratia* rather than by an intrinsic merit. In *Prisoner for God,* Dietrich Bonhoeffer commented:

> Barth was the first theologian to begin the criticism of religion—and that remains his really great merit. . . .

[Barth] called the God of Jesus Christ into the lists against religion, "*pneuma* against *sarx*." That was and is his greatest service.[4]

Perhaps because his comments on "nonreligious" Christianity and "man come of age" are fragmentary and elusive, Bonhoeffer himself was destined to exert considerable influence on recent theology. Barth offers a perspective from which secularization need not be construed as the principal antagonist for Christian faith. Bonhoeffer proceeds to suggest that the truly secular man and the Christian are one and the same:

> I have come to appreciate the "worldliness" of Christianity as never before. The Christian is not a *homo religiosus,* but a man, pure and simple, just as Jesus was man, compared with John the Baptist anyhow. . . . It is only by living completely in this world that one learns to believe.[5]

He became convinced that the premise on which Christian proclamation had traditionally been predicated was no longer valid. Man is *homo religiosus* no more, and consequently "the linchpin is removed from the whole structure of our Christianity to date."[6] Strategies that would require the conversion of secular man to religion before he could become a disciple of the Christ are not only anachronous; they also lack any real Biblical foundation. Christian faith now calls its advocates to share with its antagonists the abandonment of all religious premises.

A great many Protestant theologians have come to agree with Bonhoeffer's assessment of the individual in the modern world. Ronald Gregor Smith has written of "the new man," Helmut Gollwitzer of "areligious man," Arend van Leeuwen of "the arrival of a new type of man." In *Christianity in World History,* Van Leeuwen suggests that the technological revolution is only one aspect of a greater revolution that is rapidly destroying the cornerstone of all traditional forms of society, whether primitive or civilized —religion. In language reminiscent of Bonhoeffer, he adds that where the gospel is believed, "there is the truth accepted that there can be no returning to the age of 'religion.' "[7]

It is Friedrich Gogarten, however, who has attempted the most systematic presentation of secularization as the goal of the Biblical tradition.[8] The revelation of God in Jesus Christ means that men who have languished in bondage *to* the world are now offered the opportunity to become responsible *for* it. The Pauline denial that man can earn salvation by his works implies that all worldly activities are radically secular and devoid of religious significance. All the care and cares of the earth fall within the domain of human reason, and with their desacralization man becomes fully responsible for the world and entirely free within it.

Faith secularizes, in the sense that it enables man to move from nature into history, from dependence upon the world to autonomy. Gogarten has defined secularization as *Vergeschichtlichung der menschlichen Existenz* (man's understanding of himself becomes fully historical). He describes the new situation of the believer as one of mature sonship. The man of faith is "mature" in the sense that he acts in accordance with his own powers of rational decision, not upon instructions from others. His sonship is evident in his gratitude for the world that is his patrimony and in his awareness of the mystery of his own origin and delegated independence. The secularity of faith can be lost, however, if men either absolutize themselves and their work and drift into secular*ism* or else capitulate to any heteronomous power in the world and fall back into bondage to "the elemental spirits of the universe."

Certainly it is possible to recognize affinities between the world of the Bible and contemporary processes of secularization, even if the assertion of a direct causal relation between them, as Jacques Ellul writes in *The Technological Society,* depends merely upon "those facile, impressive,

and altogether antihistorical explanations which theorists are so fond of."[9] In *The Secular City*, for example,
Harvey Cox cites three particular motifs in the Bible that
the process of secularization presupposes. They are the
disenchantment of nature, so that it no longer seemed full
of gods, the desacralization of politics, so that no one any
longer ruled by divine right, and the deconsecration or
relativizing of human values in the light of the sovereignty
of God. In *The Relevance of Science*, the physicist C. F.
von Weizsäcker—like the philosopher Karl Jaspers—
stresses the relationship between the Christian tradition
and the assumptions that undergird the rise of modern
science in the West. But perhaps the most trenchant comments are those of Van Leeuwen, in his discussion of the
conflict between ontocratic patterns of culture and Biblical faith:

> The revolutionary history of the West up to the present
> time is rightly held to have been a continuous, ongoing
> process of secularization which nothing has been able to
> halt, let alone reverse. . . . This takes its beginning in Israel.
> Here is raised the protest against the religion of cosmic
> totality, against the "sacralizing" of all being, against the
> supremacy of fate, against the divinizing of kings and king-
> doms. Here a break is made with the everlasting cycle of
> nature and the timeless presentness of myth. Here history
> is discovered. . . . Here there is proper room for man and
> here the taste of freedom. The world is now radically secu-
> larized, becomes creation moving forward to regeneration,
> is made the arena of history.[10]

Nevertheless, there are reasons for suspicion of the
contentions that secularity is the proper Christian style for
our time or that secularization is the intention and goal of
the Biblical tradition. Precisely because secularization
denotes the most important and pervasive phenomenon
in the West since the rise of Christianity, the meaning of
the word is complex and ambiguous. Sustained conversation with disciplines other than theology is urgent, in

order that the real proportions and significance of the process of secularization might be clarified sufficiently to justify the various theological assessments that now abound. Let us raise four questions.

First, *Is secularization really as hospitable to Christian faith as Christian faith seems hospitable to secularization?* As a theological concept, secularization has often seemed strangely unrelated to some of the social realities that are commonly regarded as instances of the process. The anomaly is that the justification of secularization as a principium has often tended to inhibit the careful scrutiny of the phenomenon that would certainly enrich but might also require qualification of the endorsement. While many theologians have followed Bonhoeffer in speaking of "man come of age," possessed of a new freedom and autonomy that render anachronous old religious questions and prescriptions, those outside the theological camp often warn of the loss of freedom and autonomy that plagues man in the modern age. Perhaps we witness the maturation of a Christian process by which man moves from responsibility to the world into responsibility for it, from childhood to maturity. But perhaps the processes in which we are enmeshed are more labyrinthine, fraught with more complex dangers than our present theological vocabulary can admit. Perhaps we would do well to heed Jacques Ellul:

> Enclosed within his artificial creation, man finds that there is "no exit"; that he cannot pierce the shell of technology to find again the ancient milieu to which he was adapted for hundreds of thousands of years. The new milieu has its own specific laws which are not the laws of organic or inorganic matter. Man is still ignorant of these laws. It nevertheless begins to appear with crushing finality that a new necessity is taking over from the old. It is easy to boast of victory over ancient oppression, but what if victory has been gained at the price of an even greater subjection to the forces of the artificial necessity of the technical society which has come to dominate our lives?[11]

It is questionable whether Christian advocates of the secular have adequately explored some facets of contemporary life that appear endemic to secularization, at least insofar as we can know it now, but which seem hostile to any form of Christian faith, not merely to its religious dress. Without pretending to offer an exhaustive account, one might cite at least six aspects of secularization that require greater theological attention than they have yet received. As Thomas Luckmann reminds us, there is the progressive *privatization of freedom*. Vast sectors of Western civilization develop their own cohesive functional logic and tend to evolve autonomously. The freedom and responsibility reputed to be attributes of "man come of age" can dwindle to romantic illusions of individualism devised for private consumption in order to compensate for the loss of autonomy and agency in the public sphere. Of particular importance is the *quantification of time*, the tyranny of the clock that deprives men of spontaneity, further erodes their freedom, and imposes an alien and mechanical pattern upon the rhythms of truly human life. Time becomes a continuum in which man is ineluctably driven toward the loss of power and function, rather than a structure that always affords a "right time" for some expression of the varied cadences of life. One contemporary consequence of secularization in America is radical change in the mores of both young and old, change that testifies to the defeat of *Kairos* and the victory of *Kronos* over us all.

Perhaps no less consequential for Christian faith is the *mood of self-seriousness* that mutes our laughter, inhibits our spontaneous actions, and dulls our sense of the comic. If revelation in Christ frees man from bondage to the world so that he might become responsible for it before God, surely revelation also frees man from a sense of the irremediable seriousness of life so that he might understand it under God as a human comedy. Numerous writers have mentioned the affinities between a sense of the comic and the Christian perception of life, affinities that do not occur between the latter and the tragic vision. Few, however, have written of the conflict between this spirit and the mood of self-seriousness that attends secularization and technological progress. Such seriousness is exacerbated by the tension between putatively limitless responsibility and, because of the way that aspects of civilization develop their own autonomous logic, the suspicion that control of such power no longer lies with the rational decisions of free and responsible men. As Julian N. Hartt has written:

> Man does not get on with his proper business in a mood of unrelenting self-seriousness. Contemporary culture lays that mood upon us all. That is a major triumph of secularism as a paradoxically religious force. For if there is no one else to keep an eye on our interests we cannot afford ever to close both eyes or even to wink promiscuously. That is what I call self-seriousness. I do not of course know whether The Player can cure this disease of the spirit of modern man. Nonetheless we should send for him.[12]

If He should appear, the time of his advent will be *Kairos*. If He does not appear, we shall certainly witness the "arrival of a new type of man"—for as Johan Huizinga brilliantly argued in *Homo Ludens*, civilization in the West has been erected on and by playing. Western man is man the player. Need we not say the same of Christian man?

Three Roman Catholic philosophers have discussed three other facets of modern society, industrialized and urban, that raise scarcely less urgent questions for Christian faith in a secular time. In *The World of Silence*, Max Picard writes of the *noisiness* of an age that threatens to reduce man to no more than "a space for the noise to fill." What we euphemistically call media of communication invade the privacy of the self—with a noisiness beside which the stealth of modern techniques of information-gathering seems almost welcome—and prevent the encounter of the self with itself that is the prelude to authenticity and wholeness.

In *Leisure, the Basis of Culture,* Josef Pieper protests against the *busyness* of secularized society, most especially because Christian faith requires the sort of leisure that affords men the opportunity to see themselves and their world as a whole, not merely in terms of the functions of the self and the instrumentality of its environment. There is reason to suppose that, as the basis of the American economy has shifted from competition to cooperation, the noisiness and the busyness of life have grown more intense. Finally, Gabriel Marcel devotes *The Decline of Wisdom* to what he considers the principal danger of an instrumental approach to the world. Reason tends to diminish to the proportions of *functional reason,* so that reflection falls into discredit and both the wisdom it offers and the existential questions it raises to the light of consciousness are no longer available to men.[13] Vanished is the sense of wonder that sparks the awareness of transcendence in man's encounters with his world, with other selves, and with their ultimate source and end.

In *Religion and the Rise of Scepticism,* Franklin L. Baumer writes of a post-Christian "layman's religion" and suggests that the Christian tradition may be vanquished in its entirety by the forces cited by Picard, Marcel, and Pieper. Even as technology awards man a greater measure of "free time," the noisiness of the world and the restriction of the range of reason reduce leisure to far less than Pieper intends. But silence, reflection, and leisure are important not only for any version of faith, no matter whether religious or nonreligious, but also for any satisfactory achievement of selfhood. The human spirit cannot long survive when the self and its projects are construed in functional terms alone. The relevance of the Biblical story of Mary and Martha is not restricted to the context of traditional religion but extends to any traditional interpretation of man, no matter whether Christian or not.

In any event, if these six features of contemporary life are really endemic to secularization in the West, there is reason to qualify the current theological endorsement of the phenomenon. At least it is imperative to explore more carefully the relationship between secularization as a principium in theology and as the pervasive reality of our common life.

Implied in these reflections, of course, is a second and far broader question: *Is the secular world really as amenable to human action and humanization as many of its enthusiasts assume?* From the standpoint of moral action and reflection, the most important feature of secularization is the increasing autonomy of the various institutions within which men have to act, such as the economy and the political order. The primary social institutions no longer reside under a "sacred canopy." Instead, they tend to operate according to the functional logic of their own particular domains. Robert Nisbet has argued persuasively that technology is no longer subordinate to other human purposes. Its strides toward autonomy are analogous to developments in politics, education, and other spheres. Nisbet continues:

> The time has passed when technology needs to justify itself by its contributions to other spheres of society. Today the ends of technology are sufficient and autonomous. . . . Quite apart from its earlier ancillary function in society, technology is today an autonomous pattern of ends, functions, authorities, and allegiances.[14]

The man of action cries "Who's in charge?" The only answer is the echo of his own voice.

Therefore, the current malaise in Christian social ethics: it is difficult to direct or even to understand the real meaning of action in the context of such an autonomous area. Some writers call for the renewal of a traditional Christian world view. Others are content to applaud the idea of autonomy but demonstrate little awareness of its ambiguity. Still others have confined their attention to the private sphere. But none have persuasively resolved the essential problem: How does one understand God's purposes for man in and through these autonomous institutions and respond to Him?

Twentieth-century Protestant thought has often tended to stress the limits of man and the boundary situations in which he finds himself—especially under the impact of existentialism. But many theologians of the 1960's have looked in different directions. They have emphasized the possibilities of human life and action rather than the restrictions upon them, and the public and social aspects of man's responsibility rather than the private and personal.[15] Such is the image of man in the "death of God" theology, secular theology, the theology of hope, and political theology. But does not this perspective assume too much about the amenability of primary institutions to human action and humanization?

There are divergent opinions among the sociological theorists who contribute to this debate. For Luckmann, secularization of the public sphere is "genuinely ambivalent" because it implies "dehumanization." Talcott Parsons, however, stresses the positive aspects of our newly "differentiated" industrial society. He understands it as still a recognizably Christian affair, because of what he regards as its institutionalization of Christian values. But the voices of those who dissent from this are many, various, and highly audible in our academic preserves today.

Third, *Is secularization really antagonistic toward religion in every way?* Parsons argues that secularization involves a differentiation of roles that is consequential for religion but not intrinsically hostile to it. Robert Bellah describes something of the proportions of an American civil religion nourished on secular soil. Luckmann writes of the emergence of an invisible religion that flourishes within the privacy of the self and that is a sort of rebel-

lious stepchild of the process of secularization. Even in an
ostensibly secularized society both individual and social
forms of religiosity tend to proliferate. The use of traditional religious language within some of these forms suggests that such a vocabulary retains its cogency still, at
least from the perspectives of psychological effect and
social functionality. Whether it retains its theological
validity is, of course, another question, but one that
theologians would be well warned not to answer simply
by allusions to "irrelevance."

The presence of a powerful civil religion in America,
our Pelagian faith in education, the romantic religiosity of
dissenting movements that assume a phoenix will flutter
from every pile of ashes, our celebration of the divinity of
power, our sacralizing of the medical profession, our cos-
metic impulse and faith in drugstore magic, the *vestigia
religionis* imbedded in cliché and folklore and mythology
about sex, the gnosticism involved in some of our reliance
upon drugs, and the Manichaean stance toward life evident especially in our political affairs—these as well as
the protestations of the churches testify that America is
religious still. There is massive evidence to suggest that
the secular city is not inhospitable to religion, that the
question of whether man remains *homo religiosus* has yet
to be resolved, and that there is reason indeed to understand much of the mission of the church as a venture in
exorcism.

But the mention of exorcism raises a further question.
Can the potential demon of civil religion, for example,
be domesticated consistently except in the name of another religion that aspires to more universal community?
Can religion be exorcised except in the name of religion
itself? The unquenchable desire for ritual, for the adorn-
ment of life, for holy days and myth and symbol, for celebration that lifts man above his instrumental world and
functional understanding of himself—will these continue
to demand some form of religious expression? If that de-

mand is not satisfied by the Christian tradition, will it then issue in other varieties of piety that render life less than human, fostering expectations that can never be realized and warping discernment of self and world?

Perhaps the most pervasive form of idolatry in America is the idolatry of other selves and of images of the self. The cure for the tyranny of such images does not lie in sober recollection of the frailty of man. It can be found only within the domain of the imagination and in another constellation of images, perhaps ones such as those furnished by the sacramental and liturgical aspects of Christian faith. The sacrament of the Eucharist, for example, functions to liberate persons from the consequences of the idolatry of other selves. It offers a way of transition from the child's broken faith in the father as divine to the man's acknowledgment of the divine as father.

At this juncture, however, it is scarcely possible to evade another question. Must the future of Christianity as a religion be defended upon merely prudential grounds, and therefore provide a further instance of the triumph of functional reason, or has it some theological justification?[16] The juxtaposition of religion against Christian faith does not provide satisfactory principles of interpretation for much of the Bible. In both Old Testament and New, religion is understood as a means through which God discloses his nature and will. It is the guardian of revelation and the matrix for further divine disclosure.[17]

God is at work in the contemporary world, but divine activity does not validate itself as such. Christians believe that because he is the Father of Jesus his works continue to display a Christic form, but that form is not manifest to the casual glances of passersby.[18] Religious practices represent the incarnation and the way of the cross. They are intended to acquaint the believer so intimately with the Christ that he will be able to recognize the Christic shape involved in whatever God is doing in the present age. If there is continuity between what God once did and what he is doing now, the religious tradition with which he once identified himself will still function to enable men to recognize his presence among the many agents at work in the world. If revelation liberates men from the divinities of this world and the varieties of religion they inspire, is it not also true that from a Christian perspective religion is necessary for the deciphering of the revelation? Theologians can learn much from contemporary poets and novelists about the importance of liturgical and Scriptural detail for the interpretation of the secular city.

So, in theological perspective, secularization seems a paradoxical affair indeed. Christian faith seems to constrain its adherents to be skeptical of secularization precisely because the whole phenomenon is *too* hospitable to religion, and especially to forms of religion that are particularly vicious because they are so often covert rather than acknowledged. On the other hand, Christian faith seems to constrain its adherents to be skeptical of secularization precisely because it is *not* hospitable to the forms of religion that Christians may require for the deciphering of the contemporary divine work. Now would be a poor hour to lose the code, as the Lord struggles for and with man to preserve the fragile and precarious humanity of man—imperiled by busyness, by noisiness, by the decline of reflection, and especially by the quantification of time, the privatization of freedom, and (Can one wonder or blame?) the loss of a sense of the comic.

In the issue of whether secularization and religion are in every way hostile, our fourth and final question is implied: *Is it true that* homo religiosus *is rapidly becoming extinct?* In the contemporary American way of life there are such numerous traces of religiosity that one might argue that religion and various surrogates for it enjoy greater prominence than they did thirty or forty years ago. The comments of Bellah and Luckmann on the hardiness of civil religion and the pervasiveness of invisible religion suggest that it may still be somewhat premature to hail "the arrival of a new type of man." Whether his advent would be a matter for pure rejoicing is a different question. Certainly the Christian faith has a stake in the extinction of many and various forms of religion, but it is, after all, an interest that may be subject to serious qualification.[19]

In "Unbelief and the Secular Spirit," Langdon Gilkey contends that when modern secular man reflects upon his own characteristic attitudes, he discovers the traditional religious questions implied within them. Man's experiences of contingency, relativity, temporality, and autonomy—all these "contain latent within themselves certain disturbing and inescapable dilemmas, which point beyond the realm of the secular."[20] Perhaps the individualism and metaphysical language of earlier versions of the Christian message are no longer valid. But guilt, bondage, suffering, and death remain problems for every man, and their terror is often heightened by the processes of social change. The secularization of life, as Julian Hartt notes, enforces upon us in new ways some ancient questions that have unavoidable ontological dimensions and demand answers in terms of the individual human self.

Perhaps we can expect, then, not the death but the transfiguration of religion. There is much that is persuasive in Bellah's argument for the persistence of religion, even though the forms may vary greatly: "Man is as problematic as ever, and inescapable problems of meaning continue to confront him. The process of secularization involves a change in the structure and role of religion rather than the end of religion itself."[21]

One matter, however, is scarcely problematical: discussions of secularization will be far more cogent if they are conducted in more intimate relation to sociology. One could argue that theology is an isolated and independent exercise. But such a contention would be rash, indeed. Christian writers use the concept of secularization as both a theological principle and a description of empirical reality. Its theological usage can scarcely resolve the question of its empirical accuracy. Perspectives such as sociology affords simply cannot be ignored. Peter Berger properly contends: "Sociology . . . raises questions for the theologian to the extent that the latter's positions hinge on certain socio-historical presuppositions."[22]

It is one thing to suggest that theology must rely upon sociological analyses of secularization; it is another to delineate procedures for the appropriation of the latter. The social sciences too often have been approached simply for the benefits of the conclusions of their research. But these cannot satisfactorily be divorced from their theoretical matrix—as the disparate conclusions of Luckmann and Bellah illustrate. Their reports on private and public forms of religion depend upon theoretical perspectives and definitions that profoundly influence their analyses. While both draw upon Émile Durkheim, they appropriate this material with different emphases. Bellah assumes that every society has a specifiable religious dimension; Luckmann equates religion with every form of transcendence that is involved in distinctively human life.[23]

Sociological theory, then, may be as important for the theologian as are empirical analyses and conclusions.[24] The divergence in theory in this volume does not, of course, preclude united opposition to certain interpretations of secularization. But the theoretical differences continue to exist and, at very least, can produce salutary discussion. There are some who contend that another salvo in the battle about secularization is wasted, for theologians have begun to march on to the cadence of other issues. But we must be vigilant lest that march become more retreat than advance. Theology and ethics must still inquire into the shape of the modern world, its institutions and styles of life, its culture and its pieties. Secularization will not be retired—neither the word nor the reality.

The Meanings of Secularization

I

ABOUT THE ONLY THING that can be said with certainty of the concept of secularization is that one can seldom be certain of exactly what is meant by it. Despite its impressive ambiguity, it continues to be a central term in current sociological and theological discussion. The aim of the present essay is to attempt to clarify the concept of secularization by exhibiting the major types of concept and assessing their usefulness as theoretical guides to research.

Since the works of *Stallmann* and *Lübbe* on the history of the term "secularization" are readily available, it will be sufficient for our purposes to draw attention to a few of the implications of its rather checkered career. Already at the time of the Vulgate the Latin *saeculum* had achieved considerable ambiguity. There it bears both the religiously neutral sense of an immeasurably great span of time (*in saecula saeculorum*, I Tim. 11:17) and the religiously negative sense of "this" world which is under the power of Satan (e.g., *Et nolite conformari huic saeculo*, Rom. 12:2). In the Middle Ages the idea of "this" world has itself been neutralized to some extent so that the concept of "secular" clergy or the "secular" arm bears no connotation of hos-

From *Internationales Jahrbuch für Religionssoziologie* (Westdeutscher Verlag, 1967). Reprinted with permission of the publisher and the author.

tility to religion. The same is largely true of the first appearance of the term "secularization," which signified simply the transfer of lands and possessions from the church to the princes (Treaty of Westphalia). It is only later, especially in the French Revolution, that the expropriation of the goods of the church became an actual political program. From there it was only a short step for secularization to become the name of a program aimed at the totality of life and experience, and subsequently to assume the status of an "ism" (e.g., G. J. Holyoake's organization to promote "secularism"). Side by side with this aggressively programmatic meaning of "secularism" there has also grown up a usage which defines secularism as an attitude of indifference to religious institutions and practices or even to religious questions as such. The historical sediment of most of these past meanings still clings to "secularism" and "secularization" as they are employed today in ordinary discourse. Clearly, however, the connotations of indifference, anti-clericalism and irreligion are dominant, reflecting the long struggle in almost every area of life against the tutelary function of the churches and the Christian world view. Beginning with *Max Weber* and *Ernst Troeltsch* "secularization" was used as a descriptive and analytical term but as yet there is no agreement as to what meaning it should have in sociological theory.

II

The five concepts of secularization discussed below are ideal types presented in terms of a brief definition which describes the kind of process envisaged and its logical culmination. Following each definition one or two examples are given before a critical assessment is attempted.

1. Secularization is conceived as the decline of religion. The religious doctrines, values, and institutions which once dominated or informed the society lose their status and influence. The culmination of this kind of seculariza-

tion would be a society without religion in either an institutional or personal form. *J. Milton Yinger*, for example, terms secularization the process "in which traditional religious symbols and forms have lost force appeal."[1]

There are innumerable historical and sociological references to secularization conceived in this way. In their Middletown studies the *Lynds* measure the secularization of marriage on the basis of how many marriages were performed before ministers in 1923 as compared with 1890.[2] *John T. Flint* sets out to show that the clergy in Norway have undergone continuous secularization since the tenth century, as demonstrated in a gradual decline in prestige and their increasing isolation from the rest of society.[3] Perhaps the most comprehensive statement of the decline thesis is to be found in the work of *Pitirim A. Sorokin*. He marshals an impressive succession of statistics and observations in an effort to show that Christianity has lost its institutional and ideological dominance in Western culture. On the score of values and beliefs he argues that what was once unconditional, God-given, and absolute has become conditional, man-made, and relative.[4] On the institutional side he sees a progressive loss in authority and influence on the part of the churches and a pattern of loss in vitality and spirituality on the part of the sects.[5]

Although the "decline" thesis is one of the most widely accepted meanings of secularization and has spawned a major share of empirical research (e.g., religious practice), it is also one of the most imprecise. The difficulties in applying it stem from the ambiguities of most measures of decline and the lack of clarity as to what state or status of religion marks the norm from which decline is measured. One of *Sorokin*'s measures, for example, is the percentage of "religious" as opposed to "secular" art. But how does one actually distinguish the two? *Tillich* once referred to *Picasso*'s "Guernica" as one of the greatest modern religious paintings even though there is nothing of conventional religious subject matter about it. By contrast one

could conceivably call some Renaissance Madonnas secular because the artist's main concern seems to be perspective and composition.

An even more disconcerting question in relation to the
decline thesis is the problem of when and where we are to
find the supposedly "religious" age from which the decline
has commenced. *David A. Martin* has noted that even
secularists tend to take a utopian view of medieval religious life.[6] And *Gabriel Le Bras* has come down hard on
those who speak too easily of a "dechristianized" France.
Although there has been a decrease in conventional forms
of religious practice in France, *Le Bras* points out that
there were in former times built-in premiums and liabili-
ties relating to religious practice which may have produced large-scale conventional acceptance of Christianity
but little depth. *Le Bras* argues that in so-called dechristianized France today there are, among practicing Catholics, probably more who participate voluntarily, faithfully,
and with an understanding of what they are doing than
there were before 1789.[7] And one might add that even
though some sociologists may think the distinction between genuine and spurious expressions of a religious tradition is irrelevant to their work, the protest which has
been made since the time of *Kierkegaard* against the in-
sipidity and deceit of an "official" and "successful" Christianity is itself a fact which cannot be ignored.

2. Secularization is conceived as conformity with the
world. The religious group increasingly turns its attention
from the supernatural and the next life and becomes more
and more preoccupied with and similar to the surrounding society. The culmination of secularization in this sense
would be a religious group indistinguishable from society.
Harold Pfautz has defined secularization as "the tendency
of sectarian religious movements to become both part of
and like 'the world.' "[8]

The classic statement of this position is *Adolf Harnack*'s
characterization of the early church's growth in numbers

and wealth, its emerging hierarchical organization, and its involvement with Greek thought as a "secularization." The apex of this secularizing process, according to Harnack, was finally reached by the Jesuits under whom the church "has become specifically and definitively secularised; she opposes to the world, to history and civilization, *her own* worldly possessions."[9] In a similar argument *Pfautz* generalizes that the movement across the continuum cult-sect-institutionalized sect-church-denomination is a secularization because it involves a constant increase in size, complexity, and rationalization of structures and of modes of participation.[10]

The question which must be raised in regard to the idea of secularization as conformity with the world is whether something integral to the particular religious tradition involved is being surrendered or whether the change may not be compatible with some elements of the tradition hitherto ignored or minimized. As far as the early church or the post-Reformation sects are concerned the apparent compromise with the world may be part of a necessary differentiation within the group in order to cope with growth in size, a differentiation which may leave behind the affectional relationships of the beginning and yet not be counter to the essential thrust of the movement. Many of the changes *Pfautz* cites would occur with any small voluntary association if it began to grow in numbers and territorial location. And as far as the early church is concerned, the only way it could have avoided the "secularization" *Harnack* complains of would have been to renounce its universalism and missionary drive.

It is not enough, however, for us simply to point out the difficulties attendant on the views of secularization as "decline" or "conformity with the world." An alternative hypothesis must be advanced to account for what appears to be a generalized decline or a surrender to the surrounding society. In an important essay entitled "Christianity and Modern Industrial Society" *Talcott Parsons* suggests that what has been called secularization by *Sorokin* and others may actually be a matter of differentiation. Although the church and the Christian world view have had to give up many functions they once performed, this has been as much the result of the increasing complexity and specialization in our society as it has of a continuous falling away from the religious tradition. Moreover, although the church has resisted the loss of these functions, the basis for a differentiation of the community of faith from the general social community was already present in Christianity itself. *Parsons* concludes that the Western religious tradition has not been headed on a steady decline nor have the churches simply sold out to Mammon, but they have come to play an altered role just as many other institutions such as the family have altered their roles in keeping with the general differentiation of society.[11] As will become apparent below, the differentiation theory has considerable similarity with the concept of secularization as the disengagement of society from religion.

Although the three types of concept which follow have not been used as widely in empirical research as the two above, they are worth delineating with equal detail since they are more descriptive and also more suggestive in terms of the relationship between religious change and other variables.

3. Secularization is conceived as the desacralization of the world. The world is gradually deprived of its sacral character as man and nature become the object of rational-causal explanation and manipulation. The culmination of secularization would be a completely "rational" world society in which the phenomenon of the supernatural or even of "mystery" would play no part. Historian *Eric Kahler* writes that secularization has meant "that man became independent of religion and lived by reason, face to face with objectified, physical nature."[12]

The classical statement of this view is *Max Weber's* concept of "disenchantment" (*Entzauberung*), which signifies an irreversible trend of rationalization leading to a view of the world as a self-contained causal nexus.[13] Among contemporary writers *Mircea Eliade* has given us the most sensitive evocation of the loss (or suppression) of the sense of the sacred. *Eliade* too finds the root of desacralization in science which has so neutralized nature and human life that no point can have "a unique ontological status" which integrates the whole.[14] The proponents of the desacralization thesis do not agree as to how far this process can go. Some apparently feel that it will one day complete itself and religion, insofar as it is bound to an acknowledgment of the "sacred" or "holy," will disappear. Others hold that man is "incurably religious" and believe that either the sense of the sacred has been pushed into the unconscious for the time being or that it is in the process of finding new forms of expression.

Although less global and simplistic, the desacralization concept has certain similarities to the decline thesis. The inherent problem with the desacralization view is its assumption that religion is inextricably bound up with an understanding of the world as permeated by sacred powers. There is in Hebraic religion, however, a definite desacralization of the world through the radical transcendence of the Creator who alone is eminently holy and who has, moreover, given the world over to the dominion of man (Gen. 1:24). In Christianity the process is carried further through the separation of religion and politics and the notion of sonship through Christ in which man is free from the elemental spirits of the universe (Mark 12:17 and Gal. 4:1 ff.). This phenomenon of a religious tradition which itself desacralizes the world suggests that the desacralization view of secularization is not applicable to the Western tradition—at least in its usual form. One could apply the desacralization view to the West, however, if it were agreed that Christian faith (vs. Christianity) is not a religion but in fact the end of human religiosity.

4. Secularization is conceived as the disengagement of society from religion. Society separates itself from the religious understanding which has previously informed it in order to constitute itself an autonomous reality and consequently to limit religion to the sphere of private life. The culmination of secularization in this sense would be a religion of a purely inward character influencing neither institutions nor corporate action, and a society in which religion made no appearance outside the sphere of the religious group. The French theologian and social analyst *Roger Mehl* defines secularization as the "historical process which tends to contest the public role of religion, to substitute other forms of authority for religious authority, and finally to relegate religion to the private sector of human existence."[15]

This understanding of secularization has been investigated primarily by historians and it is seen as taking two forms, one intellectual-existential, the other institutional-social. The institutional secularization is usually traced in terms of the rise of the "secular" state and its gradual assumption of the educational and welfare functions once performed by the church. The concomitant social transformation has been analyzed in various ways. *Bernhard Grotheuysen* suggests that during the early modern period the middle class became secularized through their absorption in transforming the world through capital and technology.[16] *Dietrich von Oppen* speaks of the passing of "institutions" which participated in the holy and were an end in themselves and the rise of "organizations" that are human arrangements having no deeper dimension than the immediate purpose for which they are formed.[17] The intellectual-existential aspect of disengagement has probably been as extensively explored as any phenomenon of secularization. *Grotheuysen* aptly describes the process as "the attempt to establish an autonomous sphere of knowledge purged of supernatural, fideistic presuppositions."[18]

Although more precise than the thesis of a decline or conformity to the world, the concept of secularization as disengagement suffers from some parallel handicaps. As in the previous cases we have considered, what is referred to as disengagement or the privatizing of religion is not an unambiguously negative phenomenon. One must be careful, for example, not to exaggerate the unity of medieval society, especially to the point of overlooking the separation of the rule of Caesar and Christ which was present in Christianity from the beginning. Here again the concept of differentiation may help in neutralizing some of the negative implications of the disengagement thesis. Seen as a gradual unfolding of the theological principle of differentiation implicit in Christianity itself and the sociological principle of differentiation implicit in the development of a complex technological society, the movement toward social and intellectual autonomy appears as the logical outcome of a central stream of the Christian tradition. In the light of the negative implications of the disengagement thesis with its emphasis on autonomy from religion as such, it might be best to substitute the term "differentiation."

5. Secularization is conceived of as the transposition of beliefs and patterns of behavior from the "religious" to the "secular" sphere. In the case of disengagement and differentiation the institutions or social arrangements which are secularized are seen as something which did not necessarily belong to the sphere of religion, whereas in the case of transposition it is aspects of religious belief or experience themselves which are shifted from their sacral context to a purely human context. The culmination of this kind of secularization process would be a totally

anthropologized religion and a society which had taken over all the functions previously attaching to the religious institutions. *Trutz Rendtorff* offers as one possible meaning of secularization "the realizing in society . . . and separated from its original context . . . of the Christian inheritance."[19]

Although it is difficult to find examples of "pure" transpositions with no admixture of other ideas or experience, some well-known theses have proposed the "spirit of capitalism" as a secularization of the Calvinist ethic, the Marxist vision of the consummation of the revolution from Jewish-Christian eschatology, psychotherapy from confession and the cure of souls, etc. The classical treatment of transposition comes from *Ernst Troeltsch,* who spoke of "the complete severance of sexual feelings from the thought of original sin" which has been effected "by modern art and poetry" as "nothing else than the secularization of the intense religious emotions."[20] In another work he speaks of the belief in progress as a "secularization of Christian eschatology."[21]

The difficulty with the transposition thesis, of course, is the problem of identifying survivals or transmigrations. Is a supposed transposition really a Jewish or Christian belief or practice now appearing under the guise of a more generalized rationale, or is it something of separate origin and conception which has taken over some of the functions of the former religious phenomenon? We need only call to mind the sharp debate over the *Weber* thesis to envisage the kind of disagreements which can beset any particular thesis regarding a transposition. The widespread view that Marxism contains a transposition of some Jewish-Christian elements has also come under heavy attack.[22]

Our typological discussion would be incomplete if we did not mention two other conceptual distinctions which must be kept in mind in any consideration of the meanings of secularization. The first is the widely accepted distinction between secularization and secularism. Although more popular among theologians than social scientists, the distinction does turn up in sociological writings. Basically the contrast attempts to make secularization the reflection of a neutral attitude toward religious traditions and secularism the reflection of an antireligious program. Thus a "secular" (secularized) state would be tolerant of all religions and of irreligion but would scrupulously avoid insofar as consonant with the common good any action inimical to religious activity. A "secularistic" (sponsoring secularism) state would set out to restrict and perhaps ultimately supplant existing religions by an ideology which claims to be beyond religion because "rational," "positive," "humanistic," or "scientific."

The remaining distinction is the utterly basic one between the "secular" and the "religious." Some of the criticisms of the secularization concepts discussed above were obviously based on the suggestion that a too conventional and ill-defined "secular-religious" polarity has been assumed. *Glock* and *Stark* have pointed out that one's notion of secularization will depend on what is seen as essential to religion in general or to a particular religious tradition.[23] In relation to the polarity which lies behind most Western discussions *Niyazi Berkes* has called attention to the fact that it is based on a "Church-State" model which presupposes an institutionalized religion distinct from the political order but that this "spiritual-temporal" polarity will falsify data from non-Western cultures where such a differentiation did not originally exist. However, to enter into the actual debate over how one may redefine the "secular-religious" polarity in such a way as to make it more appropriate is quite beyond the scope of the present essay.[24] I hope it is clear from our previous discussion of the problems involved in defining secularization that this fundamental polarity is quite ambiguous and must be completely rethought.

III

One conclusion which might seem to be imposed by our analysis so far is that the term "secularization" should be dropped entirely. During its long development it has often served the partisans of religious and antireligious controversy and has constantly taken on new meanings without completely losing the old ones. As a result it is swollen with overtones and implications, especially those associated with indifference or hostility to religion. *Trutz Rendtorff* has even suggested that the uses of the concept are a more interesting subject for sociological analysis than the attempt to apply it.[25] The accumulation of connotations would be enough of a handicap, but there is an even more serious one in the fact that so many different processes and phenomena are designated by it. Often the same writer will use it in two or more senses without acknowledging the shift of meaning.

Since a moratorium on any widely used term is unlikely to be successful, there are two ways of salvaging "secularization" as a concept useful in empirical research. One, of course, is for everyone who employs it to state carefully at the beginning what meaning he intends and then stick to it. The other is to agree on a general designation which would allow it to serve as large-scale concept for certain aspects of religious change. Three of the processes discussed above could be embraced significantly by the term "secularization" since they are not contradictory or competing but complementary: desacralization, differentiation, and transposition. To a certain degree they can also be seen as representing successive and overlapping emphases in Western religious history. Although the desacralization of nature and history, for example, seems to have generally preceded political and social differentiation, the former was not accomplished all at once. And it is evident that transposition cannot take place without the prior or concomitant occurrence of differentiation. To work out the exact bearing and the measurement criteria for these subconcepts is a task that still requires considerable reflection. One of the most important aspects of this reflection, as I indicated above, will be to clarify the meaning of "religion" in each case. Just as "secularization" could be used as a higher level abstraction for three subprocesses, so "religion" could be used to cover various subcategories appropriate to desacralization, differentiation, and transposition.

Christianity and Modern Industrial Society

BECAUSE only the last half of this exceedingly important essay by Professor Talcott Parsons is reprinted here, a few introductory comments are needed. These clarify the context and the theoretical concepts which are essential for an interpretation of the argument.

The article first appeared in a *Festschrift* for Pitirim A. Sorokin, who understands its problem quite differently.[1] He discerns in the West a general decline in religiousness. This secularization involves the development from an ideational, to an idealistic, to a sensate cultural orientation, which characterizes our society. Parsons contends, however, that what has occurred in the West is not secularization as the diminution of the influence of religious values but differentiation and, indeed, the "Christianizing" of society.

Some major theoretical issues are at stake in this debate. First, what factors constitute a religious orientation? Sorokin tends to equate religiousness and otherworldliness; asceticism and mysticism are dominant in religiousness. Parsons, following Weber, insists that one must distinguish two religious orientations: otherworldly and innerworldly. Although the former leads to rejection of the world, the latter leads to "mastery over the world in the name of religious values." Sorokin's failure to admit such a distinction shapes his whole analysis. For him the primary ethical component of religiousness is the pure, spontaneous, selfless act of love. For Parsons the crucial matter is the "institutionalization of Christian ethics to become part of the structure of society itself."[2]

The second theoretical issue has already been suggested: differentiation that can take place within the religious system (e.g., faith and love) or between the religious and nonreligious elements in a more general system of action (e.g., church and social order). Differentiation does not undermine the influence of religious values although it does change the forms and means of influence. Despite tensions and countertendencies, the Christian church has most often distinguished itself from the social order, which it nevertheless has interpreted as subject to Christian values. The implementation of these values has been increasingly transferred to distinctly secular offices and activities. The "Christianizing" of secular society has been effected by the church's "influence on a life which remained by the church's own definition secular . . . but still potentially at least quite definitely Christian."[3]

Parsons' analysis of this development in the early and medieval periods has been omitted. Nevertheless, the direction of his historical analysis becomes quite clear in his interpretation of the Reformation and denominational phases.

THE REFORMATION PHASE

Perhaps the most important principle of the relation between religion and society which was institutionalized in the Middle Ages was that of the *autonomy* of secular society, of the "state" in the medieval sense, relative to the church, but within a Christian framework. The Christianity of secular society was guaranteed, not by the subjection of secular life to a religious law, but by the *common* commitment of ecclesiastical and temporal personnel to Christian faith. The Reformation may be seen, from one point of view, as a process of the extension of this principle of autonomy[4] to the internal structure of religious organization itself, with profound consequences both for the structure of the churches and for their relation to secular society. It may be regarded as a further major step in the same line as the original Christian break with Judaism.

The essential point may be stated as the religious "en-

From *Sociological Theory and Modern Society*, by Talcott Parsons. Copyright © 1967 by The Free Press, a Division of The Macmillan Company. Reprinted with permission of The Macmillan Company.

franchisement" of the individual, often put as his coming to stand in a direct relation to God. The Catholic Church had emancipated the individual, as part of its own corporate entity, from the Jewish law and its special social community, and had given him a notable autonomy within the secular sphere. But within its own definition of the religious sphere it had kept him under a strict tutelage by a set of mechanisms of which the sacraments were the core. By Catholic doctrine the only access to Divine grace was through the sacraments administered by a duly ordained priest. Luther broke through this tutelage to make the individual a *religiously* autonomous entity, responsible for his own religious concerns, not only in the sense of accepting the ministrations and discipline of the church but also through making his own fundamental religious commitments.

This brought faith into an even more central position than before. It was no longer the commitment to accept the particularized obligations and sacraments administered by the Church, but to act on the more general level in accordance with God's will. Like all reciprocal relationships, this one could be "tipped" one way or the other. In the Lutheran case it was tipped far in what in certain senses may be called the "authoritarian" direction; grace was interpreted to come only from the completely "undetermined" Divine action and in no sense to be dependent on the performances of the faithful, but only on their "receptivity." In this sense Lutheranism might be felt to deprive the individual of autonomy rather than enhancing it. But this would be an incorrect interpretation. The essential point is that the individual's dependence on the *human* mediation of the church and its priesthood through the sacraments was eliminated and *as a human being* he had, under God, to rely on his own independent responsibility; he could not "buy" grace or absolution from a human agency empowered to dispense it. In this situation the very uncertainties of the individual's relation to God, an uncertainty driven to its extreme by the Calvinistic doctrine of predestination, could, through its definition of the situation for religious interests, produce a powerful impetus to the acceptance of individual responsibility. The more deeply felt his religious need, the sharper his sense of unworthiness, the more he had to realize that no human agency could relieve him of his responsibility; "mother" church was no longer available to protect and comfort him.

An immediate consequence was the elimination of the fundamental distinction in moral-religious quality between the religious life in the Catholic sense and life in secular "callings." It was the individual's direct relation to God which counted from the human side, his faith. This faith was not a function of any particular set of ritual or semi-magical practices, or indeed even of "discipline" except in the most general sense of living according to Christian principles. The core of the special meaning of the religious life had been the sacramental conception of the earning of "merit" and this was fundamentally dependent on the Catholic conception of the power of the sacraments.

From one point of view, that of the special powers of the *church* as a social organization, this could be regarded as a crucial loss of function, and the Lutheran conception of the fundamental religious equivalence of all callings as secularization. My interpretation, however, is in accord with Max Weber's; the more important change was not the removal of religious legitimation from the special monastic life, but rather, the endowment of secular life with a new order of religious legitimation as a field of "Christian opportunity." If the ordinary man, assumed of course to be a church member, stood in direct relation to God, and could be justified by his faith, the *whole person* could be justified, including the life he led in everyday affairs. The counterpart of eliminating the sacramental mediation of the secular priesthood was eliminating also the special virtues of the religious. It was a case of further *differentiation* within the Christian framework.

Protestantism in its Lutheran phase underwent a process, analogous to that of the early church, of relative withdrawal from direct involvement in the affairs of secular society. With the overwhelming Lutheran emphasis on faith and the importance of the individual's *subjective* sense of justification, there was, as Weber pointed out, a strong tendency to interpret the concept of the calling in a passive, traditionalist, almost Pauline sense. It was the individual's relation to his God that mattered; only in a sense of nondiscrimination was his secular calling sanctified, in that it was just as good, religiously speaking, as that of the monk.

We have, however, maintained that the conception of the generalization of a Christian pattern of life was an inherent possibility in the Christian orientation from the beginning and it came early to the fore in the Reformation period in the Calvinistic, or more broadly the ascetic, branch of the movement. Here we may say that the religious status of secular callings was extended from that of a principle of basic nondiscrimination to one of their endowment with positive instrumental significance. The key conception was that of the divine ordination of the establishment of the Kingdom of God on Earth. This went beyond the negative legitimation of secular callings to the assignment of a positive *function* to them in the divine plan.

In terms of its possibility of exerting leverage over secular society this was by far the most powerful version of the conception of the possibility of a "Christian society" which had yet appeared. First, the stepwise hierarchy of levels of religious merit, so central to the Thomistic view, was eliminated by Luther. Then the individual became the focus not only of secular but also of religious responsibility emancipated from tutelary control by a sacramental church. Finally, precisely in his secular calling the individual was given a positive assignment to work in the building of the Kingdom.

The consequence of this combination was that, with one important exception, every major factor in the situation converged upon the dynamic exploitation of opportunity to change social life in the direction of conformity with religiously grounded ideals.

The basic assumption is that for Protestants the Christian commitment was no less rigorous than it had been for Catholics; if anything it was more so. In both Lutheran and Calvinistic versions the conception was one of the most rigorous submission of the individual's life to divine will. But in defining the situation for implementing this role of "creature," the Protestant position differed from the Catholic broadly as the definition of the preschool child's role relative to his parents differs from that of the school-age child's relation to his teacher. Within the family, important as the element of discipline and expectations of learning to perform are, the primary focus is on responsibility of the parents for the welfare and security of their children; the permeation of Catholic thought with familial symbolism along these lines is striking indeed.

In the school, on the other hand, the emphasis shifts. The teacher is primarily an agent of instruction, responsible for welfare, yes, but this is not the primary function; it is rather to help to equip the child for a responsible role in society when his education has been completed. To a much higher degree the question of how far he takes advantage of his opportunities becomes his own responsibility. Thus the function of the Protestant ministry became mainly a teaching function, continually holding up the Christian doctrine as a model of life to their congregations. But they no longer held a parental type of tutelary power to confer or deny the fundamentals of personal religious security.

If the analogy may be continued, the Lutheran position encouraged a more passive orientation in this situation, a leaving of the more ultimate responsibility to God, an attitude primarily of receptivity to Grace. (This is the exception referred to above—one of relatively short-run significance.) Such an attitude would tend to be generalized to worldly superiors and authorities, including both ministers and secular teachers. Ascetic Protestantism, on the other hand, though at least equally insistent on the divine origins of norms and values for life, tended to cut off this reliance on authority and place a sharper emphasis on the individual's responsibility for positive action, not just by his faith to be receptive to God's grace, but to get out and *work* in the building of the Kingdom. This precisely excluded any special valuation of devotional exercises and put the primary moral emphasis on secular activities.

Next, this constituted a liberation in one fundamental respect from the social conservatism of the Catholic position, in that it was no longer necessary to attempt to maintain the superiority of the religious life over the secular. Hence one essential bulwark of a hierarchical ordering of society was removed. The Christian conscience rather than the doctrines and structural position of the visible Church became the focus for standards of social evaluation. This should not, however, be interpreted as the establishment of "democracy" by the Reformation. Perhaps the most important single root of modern democracy is Christian individualism. But the Reformation, in liberating the individual conscience from the tutelage of the church, took only one step toward political democracy. The Lutheran branch indeed was long particularly identified with "legitimism," and Calvinism was in its early days primarily a doctrine of a relatively rigid collective "dictatorship" of the elect in both church and state.

Third, far from weakening the elements in secular society which pointed in a direction of "modernism," the Reformation, especially in its ascetic branch, strengthened and extended them. A particularly important component was clearly law. We have emphasized the essential continuity in this respect between classical antiquity and modern Europe through the medieval church. Broadly, the revival of Roman secular law in Europe was shared between Catholic and Protestant jurisdictions; in no sense did the Reformation reverse the trend in Continental Europe to institutionalize a secular legal system. In England, however, as Pound has emphasized, Puritanism was one of the major influences on the crystallization of the common law in the most decisive period. This is very much in line with the general trends of Protestant orientation, the favoring of a system of order within which responsible individual action can function effectively. The protection of rights is only one aspect of this order; the sanctioning of responsibilities is just as important.

Perhaps most important of all is the fact that the change in the character of the church meant that, insofar as the patterns of social structure which had characterized it by contrast with the feudal elements in the medieval heritage were to be preserved, they had to become much more generalized in secular society. This is true, as noted, of a generalized and codified system of law. It is true of more bureaucratic types of organization, which developed first in the governmental field but later in economic enterprise. It is by no means least true in the field of intellectual culture. The Renaissance was initially an outgrowth of the predominantly Catholic culture of Italy, but the general revival and development of learning of the post-medieval period was certainly shared by Catholic and Protestant Europe. It is a significant fact that John Calvin was trained as a lawyer. And of course, particularly in science, ascetic Protestantism was a major force in cultural development.

It is particularly important to emphasize the breadth of the front over which the leverage of Protestantism extended because of the common misinterpretation of Max Weber's thesis on the special relation between ascetic

Protestantism and capitalism. This has often been seen as though the point were that Protestantism provided a special moral justification of profit-making as such, and of that alone. In view of the deep Western ambivalence over the conception of profit, the role of ascetic Protestantism in this context could easily be interpreted as mainly a "rationalization" of the common human propensity to seek "self-interest," which is the very antithesis of religious motivation.

First, it will be recalled that Weber was quite explicit that he was not talking about profit-making in general, but only about its harnessing to systematic methodical work in worldly callings in the interest of economic production through free enterprise. Weber was also well aware of a number of other facets of the same basic orientation to work in a calling, such as its basic hostility to various forms of traditionalism, including all traditional ascription of status independent of the individual, and its relation to science, a relation much further worked out by Merton.

Even Weber did not, however, in my opinion, fully appreciate the importance of the relation to the professions as a developing structural component of modern society, a component which in certain respects stands in sharp contrast to the classical orientation of economic self-interest.

The essential point is that private enterprise in business was one special case of secular callings within a much wider context. But it was a particularly strategic case in Western development, because of the very great difficulty of emancipating economic production over a truly broad front—on the one hand from the ascriptive ties which go with such institutions as peasant agriculture and guild-type handicraft, on the other hand from the irrationalities which, from an economic point of view, are inherent in political organization, because of its inherent connection with the short-run pressures of social urgency such as defense, and because of its integration with aristocratic elements in the system of stratification which were dominated by a very different type of orientation.

There is very good reason to believe that development of the industrial revolution *for the first time* could have come about only through the primary agency of free enterprise, however dependent this was in turn on prior conditions, among the most important of which was the availability of a legal framework within which a system of contractual relations could have an orderly development. Once there has been a major breakthrough on the economic front, however, the diffusion of the patterns of social organization involved need not continue to be dependent on the same conditions.[5]

Weber's main point about the Protestant ethic and capitalism was the importance of the subordination of self-interest in the usual ideological sense to the conception of a religiously meaningful calling; only with the establishment of this component was sufficient drive mobilized to break through the many barriers which were inherent not only in the European society of the time but more generally to a more differentiated development of economic production. Basically this involves the reversal of the commonsense point of view. The latter has contended, implicitly or explicitly, that the main source of impetus to capitalistic development was the *removal* of ethical restrictions such as, for instance, the prohibition of usury. This is true within certain limits, but by far the more important point is that what is needed is a powerful motivation to innovate, to break through the barriers of traditionalism and of vested interest. It is this impetus which is the center of Weber's concern, and it is his thesis that it cannot be accounted for by any simple removal of restrictions.

However deep the ambivalence about the morality of profit-making may go, there can be little doubt that the main outcome has been a shift in social conditions more in accord with the general pattern of Christian ethics than was medieval society, provided we grant that life in this world has a positive value in itself. Not least of these is the breaking through of the population cycle of high death rates and high birth rates with the attendant lengthening of the average span of life. Another crucial point is the vast extension of the sphere of order in human relationships, the lessening of the exposure of the individual to violence, to fraud and to arbitrary pressures of authority.

So-called material well-being has certainly never been trusted as an absolute value in the Christian or any other major religious tradition, but any acceptance of life in this world as of value entails acceptance of the value of the means necessary to do approved things effectively. Particularly at the lower end of the social scale, grinding poverty with its accompaniments of illness, premature death, and unnecessary suffering is certainly not to be taken as an inherently desirable state of affairs from a Christian point of view.

Another major theme of developments in this era which is in basic accord with Christian values is a certain strain to egalitarianism, associated with the conception of the dignity of the individual human being and the need to justify discriminations either for or against individuals and classes of them in terms of some general concept of merit or demerit. Certainly by contrast with the role of ascriptive discriminations in the medieval situation, modern society is not in this respect ethically inferior.

Also important has been the general field of learning and science. Perhaps the educational revolution of the nineteenth century was even more important in its long-run implications than was the industrial revolution of the late eighteenth century. It represents the first attempt in history to give large populations as a whole a substantial level of formal education, starting with literacy but going well beyond. Associated with this is the general cultivation of things intellectual and particularly the sciences through research. It is the marriage of the educational and industrial revolutions which provides the primary basis for the quite new level of mass well-being which is one major characteristic of the modern Western world. In both developments cultures with primarily Protestant orientations have acted as the spearheads.

The Reformation phase of Western development may be said to have culminated in the great seventeenth century, which saw the foundations of modern law and political organization so greatly advanced, the culmination of the first major phase of modern science, the main orientations of modern philosophy, and much development on the economic front. However important the Renaissance was, the great civilizational achievements of the seventeenth century as a whole are unthinkable without Protestantism. It coincided with a new level of leadership centering in predominantly Protestant northern Europe, notably England and Holland, and also with much ferment in Germany.

In spite of the very great structural differences, the essential principles governing the process by which society has become more Christianized than before were essentially the same in the Reformation period as in the earlier one. Let us recall that the Christian church from the beginning renounced the strategy of incorporation of secular society within itself, or the direct control of secular society through a religious law. It relied on the common values which bound church and secular society together, each in its own sphere, but making the Christian aspect of secular society an autonomous responsibility of Christians in their secular roles. My basic argument has been that the same fundamental principle was carried even farther in the Reformation phase. The sphere of autonomy was greatly enlarged through release of the Christian individual from the tutelage of the church. This was essentially a process of further differentiation both within the religious sphere and between it and the secular.

In all such cases there is increased objective opportunity for disregarding the values of the religious tradition and succumbing to worldly temptations. But the other side of the coin is the enhancement of motivation to religiously valued achievement by the very fact of being given more unequivocal responsibility. This process was not mainly one of secularization but one of the institutionalization of the religious responsibility of the individual through the relinquishment of tutelary authority by a "parental" church.

For purposes of this discussion the Reformation period is the most decisive one, for here it is most frequently argued, by Professor Sorokin among many others, that there was a decisive turn in the direction of secularization in the sense of abandonment of the values inherent in the Christian tradition in favor of concern with the "things of this world." As already noted, we feel that underlying this argument is a basic ambiguity about the relation of "the world" to religious orientations and that the Christian orientation is not, in the Oriental sense, an orientation of "rejection of the world" but rather in this respect mainly a source for the setting of ethical standards *for* life in this world. In line with this interpretation, the Reformation transition was not primarily one of "giving in" to the temptations of worldly interest, but rather one of extending the range of applicability and indeed in certain respects the rigor of the ethical standards applied to life in the world. It was expecting more rather than less of larger numbers of Christians in their worldly lives. It goes without saying that the content of the expectations also changed. But these changes indicated much more a change in the definition of the situation of life through changes in the structure of society than they did in the main underlying values.

Let us try to apply the same formula used in summing up the medieval phase to that of the Reformation. The most conspicuous aspect of extension was the diffusion of religious responsibility and participation in certain respects beyond the sacramentally organized church to the laity on their own responsibility. The central symbol of this was the translation of the Bible into the vernacular languages of Europe and the pressure on broad lay groups to familiarize themselves with it. The shift in the functions of the church from the sacramental emphasis to that of teaching is directly connected with this. This extension included both the elements of worship and that of responsibility for ethical conduct.

With respect to the church itself as a social system, the Reformation clearly did not involve further internal differentiation but the contrary. But it involved a major step in the differentiation of the religious organization *from* secular society. The Reformation churches, as distinguished from the sects, retained their symbiosis of interpenetration with secular political authority through the principle of Establishment. But the counterpart of what I have called the religious enfranchisement of the individual was his being freed from detailed moral tutelage by the clergy. The dropping of the sacrament of penance, the very core of Luther's revolt against the Catholic Church, was central in this respect. Repentance became a matter of the individual's direct relation to God, specifically exempted from any sacramental mediation. This was essentially to say that the individual was, in matters of conscience, in principle accountable to no human agency, but only to God; in this sense he was *humanly* autonomous. This development tended to restrict the church to the functions of an agency for the generation of faith, through teaching and through providing a communal setting for the ritual expression of common anxiety and common faith.

There were two principal settings in which this differentiation of lay responsibility from ecclesiastical tutelage worked out. One was the direct relation to God in terms of repentance and faith. This was paramount in the Lutheran branch of the Reformation movement. The other was the primacy of moral action in the world as an instrument of the divine will, the pattern which was primary in ascetic Protestantism. In a sense in which this was impossible within the fold of Catholic unity on the level of church organization, both these movements become differentiated not only from the "parent" Catholic Church but also from each other. Hence the ascetic Protestant branch, which institutionalized elements present from the beginning in Western Christian tradition, notably through Augustine, was freed from the kind of ties with other components which hindered its ascendancy as the major trend of one main branch of general Christian tradition. Clearly this is the branch which had the most direct positive influence on the complex of orientations of value which later proved to be of importance to modern industrialism.

The third point of upgrading is most conspicuous in the placing of secular callings on a plane of moral equality with the religious life itself. In crucial respects this shift increased the tension between Christian ideal and world reality. This increase of tension underlay much of the Lutheran trend to withdrawal from positive secular interests and the corresponding sectarian and mystical phenomena of the time. But once the new tension was turned into the channel of exerting leverage for the change of conduct in the secular world, above all through the imperative to work in the building of the Kingdom, it was a powerful force to moral upgrading precisely in the direction of changing social behavior in the direction of Christian ideals, not of adjustment to the given necessities of a non-Christian world.

THE DENOMINATIONAL PHASE

A common view would agree with the above argument that the Reformation itself was not basically a movement of secularization but that, in that it played a part in unleashing the forces of political nationalism and economic development—to say nothing of recent hedonism—it was the last genuinely Christian phase of Western development and that from the eighteenth century on in particular the trend had truly been one of religious decline in relation to the values of secular society. Certain trends in Weber's thinking with respect to the disenchantment of the world would seem to argue in this direction, as would Troeltsch's view that there have been only three authentic versions of the conception of a Christian society in Western history—the medieval Catholic, the Lutheran, and the Calvinistic.

Against this view I should like to present an argument for a basic continuity leading to a further phase which has come to maturity in the nineteenth and twentieth centuries, most conspicuously in the United States and coincident with the industrial and educational revolutions already referred to. From this point of view, the present system of "denominational pluralism" may be regarded as a further extension of the same basic line of institutionalization of Christian ethics which was produced both by the medieval synthesis and by the Reformation.

It is perhaps best to start with the conception of religious organization itself. Weber and Troeltsch organized their thinking on these matters within the Christian framework around the distinction between church and sect as organizational types. The church was the religious organization of the whole society which could claim and enforce the same order of jurisdiction over a total population as did the state in the secular sphere. The sect, on the other hand, was a voluntary religious association of those committed to a specifically religious life. The church type was inherently committed to the conception of an Establishment, since only through this type of integration with political authority could universal jurisdiction be upheld. The sect, on the other hand, could not establish any stable relation to secular society since its members were committed to give unequivocal primacy to their religious interests and could not admit the legitimacy of the claims of secular society, politically or otherwise, which a stable relation would entail.

This dichotomy fails to take account of an important third possibility, the denomination. As I conceive it, this shares with the church type the *differentiation* between religious and secular spheres of interest. In the same basic sense which we outlined for the medieval church, both may be conceived to be subject to Christian values, but to constitute independent foci of responsibility for their implementation. On the other hand, the denomination shares with the sect type its character as a voluntary association where the individual member is bound only by a responsible personal commitment, not by *any* factor of ascription. In the American case it is, logically I think, associated with the constitutional separation of church and state.

The denomination can thus accept secular society as a legitimate field of action for the Christian individual in which he acts on his own responsibility without organizational control by religious authority. But precisely because he is a Christian he will not simply accept everything he finds there; he will attempt to shape the situation in the direction of better conformity with Christian values. This general pattern it shares with all three of the church types, but not with the sect in Troeltsch's sense.

Two further factors are involved, however, which go

beyond anything to be found in the church tradition. One of these is implicit in the voluntary principle—the acceptance of denominational pluralism—and, with it, toleration. However much there may historically have been, and still is, deep ambivalence about this problem, the genuine institutionalization of the constitutional protection of religious freedom cannot be confined to the secular side; it must be accepted as *religiously* legitimate as well. With certain qualifications this can be said to be the case in the United States today and, in somewhat more limited forms, in various other countries. From a religious point of view, this means the discrimination of two layers of religious commitment. One of these is the layer which defines the bases of denominational membership and which differentiates one denomination from another. The other is a common matrix of value-commitment which is broadly shared between denominations, and which forms the basis of the sense in which the society as a whole forms a religiously based moral community. This has, in the American case, been extended to cover a very wide range. Its core certainly lies in the institutionalized Protestant denominations, but with certain strains and only partial institutionalization, it extends to three other groups of the first importance: the Catholic Church, the various branches of Judaism, and, not least important, those who prefer to remain aloof from *any* formal denominational affiliation. To deny that this underlying consensus exists would be to claim that American society stood in a state of latent religious war. Of the fact that there are considerable tensions every responsible student of the situation is aware. Institutionalization is incomplete, but the consensus is very much of a reality.

The second difference from the church tradition is a major further step in the emancipation of the individual from tutelary control by *organized* religious collectivities beyond that reached by the Reformation churches. This is the other side of the coin of pluralism, and essentially says that the rite of baptism does not commit the individual to a particular set of dogmas or a particular religious collectivity. The individual is responsible not only for managing his own relation to God through faith *within* the ascribed framework of an established church, which is the Reformation position, but for choosing that framework itself, for deciding as a mature individual *what* to believe, and *with whom* to associate himself in the organizational expression and reinforcement of his commitments. This is essentially the removal of the last vestige of coercive control over the individual in the religious sphere; he is endowed with full responsible autonomy.

That there should be a development in this direction from the position of the Reformation church seems to me to have been inherent in the Protestant position in general, in very much the same sense in which a trend to Protestantism was inherent in the medieval Catholic position. Just as Catholics tend to regard Protestantism in general as the abandonment of true religious commitment either because the extension of the voluntary principle to such lengths is held to be incompatible with a sufficiently serious commitment on the part of the church (if you are not willing to coerce people to your point of view are you yourself *really* committed to it?) or because of its legitimation of secular society so that church membership becomes only one role among many, not the primary axis of life as a whole. But against such views it is hard to see how the implicit individualism of all Christianity could be stopped, short of this doctrine of full responsible autonomy. The doctrine seems to me implicit in the very conception of faith. Asking the individual to have faith is essentially to ask him to *trust* in God. But, whatever the situation in the relation of the human to the divine, in *human* relations trust seems to have to rest on mutuality. Essentially the voluntary principle in denominationalism is extending mutuality of trust so that no *human* agency is permitted to take upon itself the authority to control the conditions under which faith is to be legitimately expected. Clearly this, like the Reformation step, involves a risk that the individual will succumb to worldly temptations. But the essential principle is not different from that involved in releasing him from sacramental control.

This is of course very far from contending that the system of denominational pluralism is equally congenial to all theological positions or that all religious groups within the tradition can fit equally well into it. There are important strains particularly in relation to the Catholic Church, to Fundamentalist Protestant sects, to a lesser degree to very conservative Protestant church groups (especially Lutheran), and to the vestiges of really Orthodox Judaism. My essential contention is not that this pattern has been or can be fully universalized within Judaeo-Christianity, but that it is a genuinely Christian development, not by definition a falling away from religion. But it could not have developed without a very substantial modification of earlier positions within Protestantism. In particular it is incompatible with either strict traditional Lutheranism or strict Calvinism.

It was remarked above that the Reformation period did not usher in political democracy, but was in a sense a step toward it. There is a much closer affiliation between denominational pluralism and political democracy. But before discussing that, a comparison between the two may help illuminate the nature of the problem of how such a system of religious organization works. Legitimists for a long period have viewed with alarm the dangers of democracy since, if public policy can be determined by the majority of the irresponsible and the uninformed, how can any stability of political organization be guaranteed? There is a sense in which the classical theory of political liberalism may be said to play into the hands of this legitimist argument, since it has tended to assume that under democracy each individual made up his mind totally independently without reference to the institutionalized wisdom of any tradition.

This is not realistically the case. Careful study of voting behavior has shown that voting preferences are deeply anchored in the established involvement of the individual in the social structure. Generally speaking, most voters follow the patterns of the groups with which they are most strongly affiliated. Only when there are structural changes in the society which alter its structure of solidary groupings and expose many people to cross-pressures are major shifts likely to take place. There are, furthermore, mechanisms by which these shifts tend, in a well-institutionalized democratic system, to be orderly.[6]

I would like to suggest that similar considerations apply to a system of denominational pluralism. The importance of the family is such that it is to be taken for granted that the overwhelming majority will accept the religious affiliations of their parents—of course with varying degrees of commitment. Unless the whole society is drastically disorganized there will not be notable instability in its religious organization. But there will be an important element of flexibility and opportunity for new adjustments within an orderly system which the older church organizations, like the older political legitimacy, did not allow for.

If it is once granted that this system of religious organization is not by definition a "falling away" from true religion, then its institutionalization of the elements of trust of the individual has, it seems to me, an important implication. On the religious side it is implicit in the pattern of toleration. Members of particular churches on the whole trust each other to be loyal to the particular collectivity. But if some should shift to another denomination it is not to be taken too tragically since the new affiliation will in most cases be included in the deeper moral community.

But such a situation could not prevail were the secular

part of the system regarded as radically evil. The individual is not only trusted with reference to his religious participation, but also to lead a "decent" life in his secular concerns. Indeed I should argue, therefore, that for such a religious constitution to function, on the institutional level the society must present not a less but a more favorable field for the Christian life than did the society of earlier periods of Western history; its moral standards must in fact be higher.

There is a tendency in much religiously oriented discussion to assume that the test of the aliveness of Christian values is the extent to which "heroic" defiance of temptation or renunciation of worldly interests is empirically prevalent. This ignores one side of the equation of Christian conduct, the extent to which the "world" does or does not stand opposed to the values in question. If one argues that there has been a relative institutionalization of these values, and hence in certain respects a diminution of tension between religious ideal and actuality, he risks accusation of a Pharisaic complacency. In face of this risk, however, I suggest that in a whole variety of respects modern society is more in accord with Christian values than its forebears have been—this is, let it be noted, a *relative* difference; the millennium definitely has not arrived.

I do not see how the extension of intra- and interdenominational trust into a somewhat greater trust in the moral quality of secular conduct would be possible were this not so. The internalization of religious values certainly strengthens character. But this is not to say that even the *average* early Christian was completely proof against worldly temptation, *independent of any support from the mutual commitments of many Christians in and through the church*. Without the assumption that this mutual support in a genuine social collectivity was of the first importance, I do not see how the general process of institutionalization of these values could have been possible at all except on the unacceptable assumption of a process of emanation of the spirit without involvement in the realistic religious interests of real persons.

However heroic a few individuals may be, no process of mass institutionalization occurs without the mediation of social solidarities and the mutual support of many individuals in commitment to a value system. The corollary of relinquishment of the organizational control of certain areas of behavior, leaving them to the responsibility of the autonomous individual, is the institutionalization of the basic conditions of carrying out this responsibility with not the elimination, but a relative minimization of, the hazard that this exposure will lead to total collapse of the relevant standards.

Let us try to sum up this fourth—denominational— phase of the line of development we have traced in terms of our threefold formula. First I would suggest that the principle of religious toleration, inherent in the system of denominational pluralism, implies a great further extension of the institutionalization of Christian values, both inside and outside the sphere of religious organization. At least it seems to me that this question poses a sharp alternative. Either there is a sharp falling away so that, in tolerating each other, the different denominations have become fellow condoners of an essentially evil situation or, as suggested above, they do in fact stand on a relatively high ethical plane so that whatever their dogmatic differences, there is no basis for drawing a drastic moral line of distinction which essentially says that the adherents of the other camp are in a moral sense not good people in a sense in which the members of our own camp are. Then the essential extension of the same principle of mutual trust into the realm of secular conduct is another part of the complex which I would like to treat as one of extension of the institutionalization of Christian values.

So far as differentiation is concerned, there are two

conspicuous features of this recent situation. First, of course, the religious associations have become differentiated from each other so that, unlike in the Reformation phase (to say nothing of the Middle Ages), when there was for a politically organized society in principle only one acceptable church, adherence to which was the test of the moral quality treated as a minimum for good standing in the society, this is no longer true. The religious organization becomes a purely voluntary association, and there is an indefinite plurality of morally acceptable denominations.

This does not, however, mean that Christian ethics have become a matter of indifference in the society. It means rather that the differentiation between religious and secular spheres has gone farther than before and with it the extension of the individualistic principle inherent in Christianity to the point of the "privatizing" of formal, external religious commitment, as the Reformation made internal religious faith a matter for the individual alone. This general trend has of course coincided with an enormously proliferated process of differentiation in the structure of the society itself.

In this respect the religious group may be likened (up to a point) to the family. The family has lost many traditional functions and has become increasingly a sphere of private sentiments. There is, however, reason to believe that it is as important as ever to the maintenance of the main patterns of the society, though operating with a minimum of direct outside control. Similarly religion has become largely a private matter in which the individual associates with the group of his own choice, and in this respect has lost many functions of previous religious organizational types.

There seem to be two primary respects in which an upgrading process may be spoken of. Approaching the question from the sociological side, we may note that the development of the society has been such that it could not be operated without an upgrading of general levels of responsibility and competence, the acquisition and exercise of the latter of course implying a high sense of responsibility. This trend is a function of increase in the size of organization and the delicacy of relations of interdependence, of freedom from ascriptive bonds in many different ways, of the sheer power for destruction and evil of many of the instrumentalities of action.

Responsibility has a double aspect. The first is responsibility *of* the individual in that he cannot rely on a dependent relation to others, or to some authority, to absolve him of responsibility—this is the aspect we have been referring to as his *autonomy* in the specific sense in which the term has been used in this discussion. The other aspect is responsibility *for* and *to*, responsibility for results and to other persons and to collectivities. Here the element of mutuality inherent in Christian ethics, subject to a commonly binding set of norms and values, is the central concern.

That the general trend has been to higher orders of autonomous responsibility is, in my opinion, sociologically demonstrable.[7] The central problem then becomes that of whether the kinds of responsibility involved do or do not accord with the prescriptions of Christian ethics. This is essentially the question of whether the general trend stemming from ascetic Protestantism is basically un-Christian or not. Granting that this trend is not un-Christian, the critical *moral* problems of our day derive mainly from the fact that, since we are living in a more complicated world than ever before, which is more complicated because human initiative has been more daring and has ventured into more new realms than ever before, greater demands are being put on the human individual. He has more difficult problems, both technical and moral; he takes greater risks. Hence the possibility of failure and of the failure being his fault is at least as great as, if not greater than, it ever was.

There is a widespread view, particularly prevalent in religious circles, that our time, particularly some say in the United States, is one of unprecedented moral collapse. In these circles it is alleged that modern social development has entailed a progressive decline of moral standards which is general throughout the population. This view is clearly incompatible with the general trend of the analysis we have been making. Its most plausible grain of truth is the one just indicated, that as new and more difficult problems emerge, such as those involved in the possibility of far more destructive war than ever before, we do not feel morally adequate to the challenge. But to say that because we face graver problems than our forefathers faced we are doubtful of our capacity to handle them responsibly is quite a different thing from saying that, on the same levels of responsibility as those of our forefathers, we are in fact handling our problems on a much lower moral level.

Our time by and large, however, is not one of religious complacency but, particularly in the most sensitive groups in these matters, one of substantial anxiety and concern. Does not the existence of this concern stand in direct contradiction to the general line of argument I have put forward?

I think not. One element in its explanation is probably that new moral problems of great gravity have emerged in our time and that we are, for very realistic reasons, deeply concerned about them. My inclination, however, is to think that this is not the principal basis of the widespread concern.

The present discussion has, by virtue of its chosen subject, been primarily interested in the problems of the institutionalization of the values originating in Christianity as a religious movement, which have been carried forward at various stages of its development. But values—i.e., moral orientations toward the problems of life in this world—are never the whole of religion, if indeed its most central aspect. My suggestion is that the principal roots of the present religious concern do not lie in *relative* moral decline or inadequacy (relative, that is, to other periods in our society's history) but rather in problems in the other areas of religion, problems of the bases of faith and the definitions of the ultimate problems of meaning.

The very fact that the process of the integration of earlier religious values with the structure of society has gone so far as it has gone raises such problems. The element of universalism in Christian ethics inherently favors the development of a society where the different branches of Christianity cannot maintain their earlier insulation from each other. The problem of the status of Judaism has had to be raised on a new level within the structure of Western society, one which came to a very critical stage in the case of German Nazism. It is a society in which all the parochialisms of earlier religious commitments are necessarily brought into flux.

But beyond this, for the first time in history something approaching a world society is in process of emerging. For the first time in its history Christianity is now involved in a deep confrontation with the major religious traditions of the Orient, as well as with the modern political religion of Communism.

It seems probable that a certain basic tension in relation to the "things of this world" is inherent in Christianity generally. Hence any relative success in the institutionalization of Christian values cannot be taken as final, but rather as a point of departure for new religious stocktaking. But in addition to this broad internal consideration, the confrontation on such a new basis with the non-Christian world presents a new and special situation. We are deeply committed to our own great traditions. These have tended to emphasize the exclusive possession of the truth. Yet we have also institutionalized the values of tolerance and equality of rights for all. How can we define a meaningful orientation in such a world when, in addition, the more familiar and conventional problems of suffering and evil are, if not more prevalent than ever before, at least as brought to attention through mass communications, inescapable as facts of our world?

It is the inherent tension and dynamism of Christianity and the unprecedented character of the situation we face which, to my mind, account for the intensive searching and questioning, and indeed much of the spiritual negativism, of our time. The explanation in terms of an alleged moral collapse would be far too simple, even if there were more truth in it than the evidence seems to indicate. For this would imply that we did not need new conceptions of meaning; all we would need would be to live up more fully to the standards familiar to us all. In no period of major ferment in cultural history has such a solution been adequate.

THOMAS LUCKMANN

The Invisible Religion

INSTITUTIONAL SPECIALIZATION of religion, it should be noted, was part of a far-reaching historical process which transformed a traditional social order into modern industrial society. This process was characterized by a complex pattern of successive phases in which political, religious and economic institutions became increasingly specialized in their functions at the same time that the organization of the institutional areas became increasingly "rational."[1] This process led to the sharp segmentation of the several institutional domains which characterize modern industrial societies. The norms within the separate domains became increasingly "rational" in relation to the *functional* requirements of the institution.[2] The functionally "rational" norms of institutions characterized by a complex division of labor and specialization of roles became increasingly disengaged from the biographical context of meaning in which institutional performances stood for the individual performer. As was indicated earlier, the norms within the separate institutional domains gained a high degree of autonomy. The norms within an institutional domain were thus attached to clearly circumscribed, restricted jurisdictions, but retained unquestioned validity within their jurisdictions.

The church did not escape this development. She gained a high degree of internal autonomy and her institutional structure was characterized by the trend to functional rationality. The validity of her norms became restricted to a specifically "religious sphere," while the global claims of the "official" model were generally neutralized as mere rhetoric. Despite considerable similarity in the development which led to the specialization of economic, political and religious institutions, however, the process has some peculiar consequences for religion.

Institutional segmentation of the social structure significantly modifies the relation of the individual to the social order as a whole. His "social" existence comes to consist of a series of performances of highly anonymous specialized social roles. In such performances the person and the personal, biographical context of meaning become irrelevant. At the same time, the "meaning" of performances in one institutional domain, determined by the autonomous norms of that domain, is segregated from the "meaning" of performances in other domains. The "meaning" of such performances is "rational"—but only with respect to the functional requirements of a given institutional area. It is, however, detached from the overarching context of meaning of an individual biography. The missing (or poor) integration of the meaning of institutional performances into a system of *subjective* significance does not disturb the effective functioning of economic and political institutions. As an actor on the social scene the individual does not liberate himself from the control of institutional norms. Since the "meaning" of these norms only indirectly affects his personal identity and since it has only a "neutral" status in the subjective system of significance, however, the individual does escape the consciousness-shaping effect of institutional norms to a considerable extent. The individual becomes replaceable as a person in proportion to the increasing anonymity of specialized roles that are determined by the functionally rational institutions. More precisely, the subjective biographical context of the performances becomes entirely trivial from the point of view of the institutional domains. The latter need be concerned only with the effective control of performances. The functional rationality of segregated institutional norms tends to make *them* trivial from the point of view of the person who is, therefore, increasingly unlikely to offer subjective resistance to them—a resistance that might be potentially inspired by a conflict between institutional norms and a presumed religious system of significance. The segregation of "rational" institutional norms in the consciousness of the individual is the social-psychological correlate of the institutional segmentation of the social structure.

The segregation of institutionally specialized *religious* norms, however, which originates in the same global processes of social change, seriously affects the function of religious representations. The jurisdiction originally claimed by the "official" model of religion is total, in accordance with the fact that the model is intended to represent a pervasive coherence of sense in the life of the individual. No doubt the global claim of the "official" model of religion can be neutralized, as we have pointed out in the formal analysis of the different modes of internalization of the "official" model. The transformation of specifically religious representations into a system of mere rhetoric, however, necessarily undermines this social form of religion. The approximate congruence between the official model of religion and the prevalent subjective systems of "ultimate" significance is lost. We shall have to return to a discussion of some further implications of institutional specialization of religion for the individual in modern society. First, a few remarks on the general consequences of institutional segmentation are in order.

The combination of continued performance control and increasing disengagement from the person which characterizes the primary public institutions in modern industrial societies is the basis for the seeming paradox discussed today under the headings of "individualism" and "conformity." The moral and ideological fervor generated by this discussion tends to preclude an insight into the common structural source of both phenomena. In comparison to traditional social orders, the primary public institutions no longer significantly contribute to the formation of individual consciousness and personality, despite the massive performance control exerted by their functionally rational "mechanisms." Personal identity becomes, essentially, a private phenomenon. This is, perhaps, the most revolutionary trait of modern society. Institutional segmentation left wide areas in the life of the individual unstructured and the overarching biographical context of significance undetermined. From the interstices of the social structure that resulted from institutional segmentation emerged what may be called a "private sphere." The "liberation" of individual consciousness from the social structure and the "freedom" in the "private sphere" provide the basis for the somewhat illusory sense of autonomy which characterizes the typical person in modern society.

We need not discuss here the special problem of the family, beyond a few cursory remarks. The family ceased to be a primary public institution in the sense in which that term applies to political and economic institutions. As the "family of procreation" it continues to transmit meaning of overarching biographical significance—more or less successfully. As the "family of orientation" it becomes a basic and, as it were, semi-institutional component of the emerging "private sphere"—a point to which we shall return later. Another problem that cannot be taken up here is the totalitarianism appearing in some modern industrial societies. Its regressive attempts to infuse "public" norms into the "private sphere" and to shape individual consciousness on supra-individual and "irrational" models did not prove successful in the long run.

The sense of autonomy which characterizes the typical individual in modern industrial societies is closely linked to a pervasive consumer orientation. Outside the areas that remain under direct performance control by the primary institutions, the subjective preferences of the individual, only minimally structured by definite norms, determine his conduct. To an immeasurably higher degree than in a traditional social order, the individual is left to his own devices in choosing goods and services, friends, marriage partners, neighbors, hobbies and, as we shall show presently, even "ultimate" meanings in a relatively autonomous fashion. In a manner of speaking, he is free to construct his own personal identity. The consumer orientation, in short, is not limited to economic products but characterizes the relation of the individual to the entire culture. The latter is no longer an obligatory structure of interpretive and evaluative schemes with a distinct hierarchy of significance. It is, rather, a rich heterogeneous assortment of possibilities which, in principle, are accessible to any individual consumer. It goes without saying that the consumer preferences still remain a function of the consumer's social biography.

The consumer orientation also pervades the relation of the "autonomous" individual to the sacred cosmos. One highly important consequence of institutional segmentation, in general, and institutional specialization of religion, in particular, is that the specifically religious representations, as congealed in the "official" models of the churches, cease to be the only and obligatory themes in the sacred universe. From the socially determined systems of effective priorities new themes of "ultimate" significance emerge and, to the extent that they are socially articulated, compete for acceptance in the sacred cosmos. The thematic unity of the traditional sacred cosmos breaks apart. This development reflects the dissolution of *one* hierarchy of significance in the world view. Based on the complex institutional structure and social stratification of industrial societies different "versions" of the world view emerge. The individual, originally socialized into one of the "versions" may continue to be "loyal" to it, to a certain extent, in later life. Yet, with the pervasiveness of the consumer orientation and the sense of autonomy, the individual is more likely to confront the culture and the sacred cosmos as a "buyer." Once religion is defined as a "private affair" the individual may choose from the assortment of "ultimate" meanings as he sees fit—guided only by the preferences that are determined by his social biography.

An important consequence of this situation is that the individual constructs not only his personal identity but also his individual system of "ultimate" significance. It is true that for such constructions a variety of models is socially available—but none is "official" in the strict sense of the term.[3] None is routinely internalized *au sérieux*. Instead, a certain level of subjective reflection and choice determines the formation of individual religiosity—a point that was made earlier.[4] Furthermore, themes of "ultimate" significance emerge primarily out of the "private sphere" and are, on the whole, not yet fully articulated in the culture. The individual systems of "ultimate" significance tend to be, therefore, both syncretistic and vague, in comparison with an "official" model internalized *au sérieux*.

It should be noted that the traditional, specifically religious representations still form part of the heterogeneous sacred cosmos in modern society. They are, indeed, the only part of the sacred cosmos that is commonly recognized as religious. The other elements are usually described as "pseudoreligious" or are not perceived as part of the sacred cosmos, despite the fact that they may be dominant themes in the prevalent individual systems of "ultimate" significance. The specifically religious representations, furthermore, still form something not unlike a model, a model that bears some resemblance to traditional "official" models of religion. It should be remembered, however, that once the *traditional* sacred cosmos came to reside exclusively in a specialized institution, the jurisdiction of this institution and, indirectly, of the sacred cosmos, was increasingly restricted to the "private sphere." This, in turn, tended to neutralize—although, perhaps, not completely—the privileged status of the traditional "offi-

cial" model in relation to other themes of "ultimate" significance that addressed themselves to the "inner man."
The "autonomous" individual today confronts the traditional specifically religious model more or less as a
consumer, too. In other words, that model is one of the
possible choices of the individual. But even for those who
continue to be socialized into the traditional model, specifically religious representations tend to have a predominantly rhetorical status. Various studies have shown that
church-oriented religiosity typically contains only a shal-
low "doctrinal" layer consisting of "religious opinions"
which do not stand in a coherent relation to one another.[5]

The conflict between the claims of the traditional model
and the socially determined circumstances of everyday
life rarely, if ever, becomes acute—precisely because it is
generally taken for granted that these claims are rhetorical. They find no support from other institutions and fail
to receive "objective" reaffirmation in the daily lives of
the individuals.[6] The subjective neutralization of these
claims, on the other hand, makes it possible for the former
"official" model to survive as rhetoric. In the typical case,
a conscious rejection of traditional forms of religion,
merely because they are not congruent with the effective
priorities of everyday life, becomes unnecessary. The
neutralization of the claims does, however, contribute to
further dissolution of the coherence of the model and reinforces the restriction of specifically religious representations to the "private sphere."

The social location of the churches in the contemporary
industrial societies decisively influences the selection of
those social types who continue to be socialized into the
traditional "official" model and determines the manner in
which the model is likely to be internalized. Summing up
the results of research on church religion we said that the
more "modern" the constellation of factors determining
the socialization of the individual, the less likely is the
routine internalization of the model and, if internalization

still occurs, the less likely will it be *au sérieux*. But even in the case of church-oriented individuals it is likely that effective priorities of everyday life, the subjective system of "ultimate" significance and the rhetoric of the traditional "official" model are incongruent—for reasons that were already indicated. An additional reason is the sociability and prestige-substitution function which church religion may continue to perform in the lives of certain types of persons even after the specifically religious function is neutralized.

In view of this situation it is useful to regard church religiosity in two different perspectives. First, we may view church religiosity as a survival of a traditional social form of religion (that is, institutional specialization) on the periphery of modern industrial societies. Second, we may view church religiosity as one of the many manifestations of an emerging, institutionally nonspecialized social form of religion, the difference being that it still occupies a special place among the other manifestations because of its historical connections to the traditional Christian "official" model. Many phenomena of contemporary church religion make better sense if placed in the second, rather than the first, perspective.

Institutional segmentation of the social structure and the dissolution of the traditional, coherent sacred cosmos affected not only religion as a specialized institution but also the relation of the traditional, specifically religious representations to the values of other specialized institutional domains. The prevalent norms in the various institutional areas, especially economics and politics, were increasingly legitimated by functional rationality. The more autonomous and rational the specialized institutional areas became, the less intimate grew their relation to the transcendent sacred cosmos. The traditional legitimation from "above" (for example, the ethic of vocation and the divine right of kings) is replaced by legitimation from "within" (for example, productivity and independence). In this sense the norms of the institutional domains did become increasingly "secular." This does not mean, however, that the institutional domains became denuded of "values." "Secularization" in its early phases was not a process in which traditional sacred values simply faded away. It was a process in which autonomous institutional "ideologies" replaced, within their own domain, an overarching and transcendent universe of norms.

This, precisely, constitutes the key problem for the relation of the "modern" individual to the social order. In the long run, isolated institutional "ideologies" were incapable of providing a socially prefabricated *and* subjectively meaningful system of "ultimate" significance. The reasons for this inability, as we have seen, are connected with the social-psychological consequences of institutional segmentation and specialization—with the very processes, in fact, that gave rise to isolated institutional "ideologies." The fate of totalitarianism in modern industrial societies shows that attempts to transform "institutional" ideologies into encompassing world views were not notably successful. Even Communism—which articulated something like an "official" model and which succeeded in enforcing routine socialization of "everybody" into that model in the Soviet Union—seems to have failed in producing a "new man." On the whole, the post-Revolution generations seem to have internalized the "official" model as a system of rhetoric, rather than *au sérieux*. The "retreat into the private sphere," while less conspicuous than in "capitalist" countries, is clearly noticeable. The attempts to articulate a coherent and subjectively compelling world view with sacred qualities on the basis of elements taken from "institutional" ideologies (such as "free enterprise"), undertaken in the United States under such pressures as the Cold War and Korea, were doomed to fail because not even tongue-in-cheek internalization could be generally enforced.[7] Furthermore, it proved impossible to create, *ex nihilo,* an internal logic that would connect the disparate elements that went into these products.

It was pointed out earlier that the sacred cosmos of modern industrial societies no longer represents *one* obligatory hierarchy and that it is not articulated as a consistent thematic whole. It may sound like an exaggerated metaphor if one speaks of the sacred cosmos of modern industrial societies as *assortments* of "ultimate" meanings. The term points out accurately, however, a significant distinction between the modern sacred cosmos and the sacred cosmos of a traditional social order. The latter contains well-articulated themes which form a universe of "ultimate" significance that is reasonably consistent in terms of its own logic. The former also contains themes that may be legitimately defined as religious; they are capable of being internalized by potential consumers as meanings of "ultimate" significance. These themes, however, do not form a coherent universe. The assortment of religious representations—a sacred *cosmos* in a loose sense of the term only—is not internalized by any potential consumer as a whole. The "autonomous" consumer selects, instead, certain religious themes from the available assortment and builds them into a somewhat precarious private system of "ultimate" significance. Individual religiosity is thus no longer a replica or approximation of an "official" model.

We shall have to return to a discussion of the peculiar character of the sacred cosmos in modern industrial societies. These preliminary observations should suffice, however, to make us aware of the danger of oversimplification in analyzing the social basis of the modern sacred cosmos. The question, properly formulated, is, What are the social bases of the assortment of religious themes prevalent in industrial societies? Our analysis of church religion in modern society sharply pointed up the fact that the modern sacred cosmos as a whole no longer rests

on institutions specializing in the maintenance and trans-
mission of a sacred universe. On the basis of our observations on the "secular" institutional ideologies we may say,
furthermore, that the sacred cosmos as a whole does not
rest on other primary and specialized institutional areas
whose main functions are not religious—as, for example,
the state and the economic system. When we turn to a discussion of the origin of various themes in the modern
sacred cosmos we shall have occasion to point out that
some themes can be traced back to the traditional Christian cosmos and others to "secular" institutional ideologies. But this is a point that is mainly of historical interest.
The effective social basis of the modern sacred cosmos is
to be found in neither the churches nor the state nor the
economic system.

The social form of religion emerging in modern industrial societies is characterized by the direct accessibility
of an assortment of religious representations to potential
consumers. The sacred cosmos is mediated neither through
a specialized domain of religious institutions nor through
other primary public institutions. It is the direct accessibility of the sacred cosmos, more precisely, of an assortment of religious themes, which makes religion today
essentially a phenomenon of the "private sphere." The
emerging social form of religion thus differs significantly
from older social forms of religion which were characterized either by the diffusion of the sacred cosmos through
the institutional structure of society or through institutional specialization of religion.

The statement that the sacred cosmos is directly accessible to potential consumers needs to be explicated. It
implies that the sacred cosmos is not mediated by primary
public institutions and that, correspondingly, no obligatory model of religion is available. It does not imply, of
course, that religious themes are not socially mediated in
some form. Religious themes originate in experiences in
the "private sphere." They rest primarily on emotions and

sentiments and are sufficiently unstable to make articulation difficult. They are highly "subjective"; that is, they are not defined in an obligatory fashion by primary institutions. They can be—and are—taken up, however, by what may be called secondary institutions which expressly cater to the "private" needs of "autonomous" consumers. These institutions attempt to articulate the themes arising in the "private sphere" and retransmit the packaged results to potential consumers. Syndicated advice columns, "inspirational" literature ranging from tracts on positive thinking to *Playboy* magazine, *Reader's Digest* versions of popular psychology, the lyrics of popular hits, and so forth, articulate what are, in effect, elements of models of "ultimate" significance. The models are, of course, non-obligatory and must compete on what is, basically, an open market. The manufacture, the packaging and the sale of models of "ultimate" significance are, therefore, determined by consumer preference, and the manufacturer must remain sensitive to the needs and requirements of "autonomous" individuals and their existence in the "private sphere."[8]

The appearance of secondary institutions supplying the market for "ultimate" significance does not mean that the sacred cosmos—after a period of institutional specialization—is once again diffused through the social structure. The decisive difference is that the primary public institutions do not maintain the sacred cosmos; they merely regulate the legal and economic frame within which occurs the competition on the "ultimate" significance market. Furthermore, diffusion of the sacred cosmos through the social structure characterizes societies in which the "private sphere," in the strict sense of the term, does not exist and in which the distinction between primary and secondary institutions is meaningless.

The continuous dependence of the secondary institutions on consumer preference and, thus, on the "private sphere" makes it very unlikely that the social objectivation of themes originating in the "private sphere" and catering to it will eventually lead to the articulation of a consistent and closed sacred cosmos and the specialization, once again, of religious institutions. This is one of the several reasons that justify the assumption that we are not merely describing an interregnum between the extinction of one "official" model and the appearance of a new one, but, rather, that we are observing the emergence of a new social form of religion characterized neither by diffusion of the sacred cosmos through the social structure nor by institutional specialization of religion.

The fact that the sacred cosmos rests primarily on the "private sphere" and the secondary institutions catering to the latter, combined with the thematic heterogeneity of the sacred cosmos, has important consequences for the nature of individual religiosity in modern society. In the absence of an "official" model the individual may select from a variety of themes of "ultimate" significance. The selection is based on consumer preference, which is determined by the social biography of the individual, and similar social biographies will result in similar choices. Given the assortment of religious representations available to potential consumers and given the absence of an "official" model it is possible, in principle, that the "autonomous" individual will not only select certain themes but will construct with them a well-articulated private *system* of "ultimate" significance. To the extent that some themes in the assortment of "ultimate" meanings are coalesced into something like a coherent model (such as "positive Christianity" and psychoanalysis), some individuals may internalize such models en bloc. Unless we postulate a high degree of reflection and conscious deliberation, however, it is more likely that individuals will legitimate the situation-bound (primarily emotional and affective) priorities arising in their "private spheres" by deriving, *ad hoc*, more or less appropriate rhetorical elements from the sacred cosmos. The assumption seems justified, therefore,

that the *prevalent* individual systems of "ultimate" significance will consist of a loose and rather unstable hierarchy
of "opinions" legitimating the affectively determined priorities of "private" life.

Individual religiosity in modern society receives no
massive support and confirmation from the primary public
institutions. Overarching subjective structures of meaning
are almost completely detached from the functionally
rational norms of these institutions. In the absence of
external support, subjectively constructed and eclectic
systems of "ultimate" significance will have a somewhat
precarious reality for the individual.[9] Also, they will be
less stable—or rigid—than the more homogeneous patterns of individual religiosity that characterize societies
in which "everybody" internalizes an "official" model and
in which the internalized model is socially reinforced
throughout an individual's biography. In sum, while the
systems of "ultimate" significance in modern society are
characterized by considerable variability in content, they
are structurally similar. They are *relatively* flexible as well
as unstable.

While individual religiosity fails to receive the massive
support and confirmation from primary public institutions,
it comes to depend upon the more ephemeral support of
other "autonomous" individuals. In other words, individual religiosity is socially supported by other persons who,
for reasons discussed above, are found primarily in the
"private sphere." In the "private sphere" the partial sharing, and even joint construction, of systems of "ultimate"
significance is possible without conflict with the functionally rational norms of the primary institutions. The so-
called nuclear family prevalent in industrial societies
performs an important role in providing a structural basis
for the "private" production of (rather fleeting) systems
of "ultimate" significance. This holds especially for the
middle-class family ideal of "partnership marriage" of
which it is typically expected that it provide "fulfillment"

for the marriage partners.[10] If the situation is viewed in this perspective there is nothing surprising about the upsurge of "familism" in industrial societies, unexpected as this fact would have been for the social scientists of the nineteenth century. On the other hand the relatively low average stability of the family as an institution becomes readily intelligible if one allows for the extraordinarily heavy social-psychological burden that is placed upon the family by such expectations.[11]

Support for subjective systems of "ultimate" significance may also come from persons outside the family. Friends, neighbors, members of cliques formed at work and around hobbies may come to serve as "significant others" who share in the construction and stabilization of "private" universes of "ultimate" significance.[12] If such universes coalesce to some degree, the groups supporting them may assume almost sectarian characteristics and develop what we earlier called secondary institutions. This, to list only the most unlikely example, seems to be the case even with such "ultimately" significant hobbies as wife-swapping.[13] Nevertheless, it is safe to assume that the family remains the most important catalyst of "private" universes of significance.

It may be unnecessary to stress again the difficulties in defining and describing the dominant themes in the modern sacred cosmos. The main reasons for these difficulties have already been stated. The religious themes of modern industrial societies do not form a consistently and sharply articulated sacred cosmos. The dominant themes which originate in the "private sphere" are relatively unstable. To the extent that the traditional Christian rhetoric survives it provides a vocabulary that may hide newly emerging themes. Finally, the themes of "ultimate" significance are internalized in a significantly different manner in different social strata. All this makes a description of the modern sacred cosmos far more difficult than, for example, an exposition of traditional Lutheran dogma. In view of the intrinsic interest and significance of the problem, however, even a tentative sketch of what appear to be the dominant themes in the modern sacred cosmos may be justified.

The dominant themes in the modern sacred cosmos bestow something like a sacred status upon the individual by articulating his "autonomy." This, of course, is consistent with our finding that "ultimate" significance is found by the typical individual in modern industrial societies primarily in the "private sphere"—and thus in his *"private"* biography. The traditional symbolic universes become irrelevant to the everyday experience of the typical individual and lose their character as a (superordinated) reality. The primary social institutions, on the other hand, turn into realities whose sense is alien to the individual. The transcendent social order ceases to be *subjectively* significant both as a representation of an encompassing cosmic meaning and in its concrete institutional manifestations. With respect to matters that "count," the individual is retrenched in the "private sphere." It is of considerable interest that even those subordinate themes in the modern sacred cosmos that are derived from economic and political ideologies tend to be articulated in an increasingly "individualistic" manner—for example, the responsible citizen, the successful business "operator."

The theme of the "autonomous" individual has some historical antecedents, from certain elements in classical Stoicism to the philosophies of the Enlightenment. It received its first modern articulation in the Romantic era. It was then linked to a variety of other themes that ranged from notions of the "freedom of the artist" to nationalism. The theme was rooted socially in the capitalist bourgeoisie and, most conspicuously, in the bohemian fringes of the latter. With the growth and transformation of the middle classes in industrial society, however, the theme became the central topic of the modern sacred cosmos. Even where it was originally linked to a tradition of individual responsibility in a community of individuals (as in the United States) it eventually lost its "transcendent" political halo. The retrenchment of the individual in the "private sphere"—which, as we indicated presupposes a special, historically unique constellation of social-structural factors—finds a thematic parallel in the redefinition of personal identity to mean the "inner man." Individual "autonomy" thus comes to stand for absence of external restraints and traditional taboos in the private search for identity.

The theme of individual "autonomy" found many different expressions. Since the "inner man" is, in effect, an undefinable entity, its presumed discovery involves a lifelong quest. The individual who is to find a source of "ultimate" significance in the subjective dimension of his biography embarks upon a process of self-realization and self-expression that is, perhaps, not continuous—since it is immersed in the recurrent routines of everyday life—but certainly interminable. In the modern sacred cosmos self-expression and self-realization represent the most important expressions of the ruling topic of individual "autonomy." Because the individual's performances are controlled by the primary public institutions, he soon recognizes the limits of his "autonomy" and learns to confine the quest for self-realization to the "private sphere." The young may experience some difficulty in accepting this restriction—a restriction whose "logic" is hardly obvious until one learns to appreciate the "hard facts of life." Content analysis of popular literature, radio and television, advice columns and inspirational books provides ample evidence that self-expression and self-realization are prominent themes, indeed. They also occupy a central position in the philosophy, if not always the practice, of education. The individual's natural difficulty in discovering his "inner self" explains, furthermore, the tremendous success of various scientific and quasi-scientific psychologies in supplying guidelines for his search.[14]

The prevalent mobility ethos can be considered a specific expression of the theme of self-realization.[15] Self-realization by means of status achievement precludes, of course, a radical retrenchment in the "private sphere." It is significant, however, that the mobility ethos is typically linked to an attitude toward the social order which is both "individualistic" and manipulative. Finally, since there is a structurally determined discrepancy between the mobility ethos and status achievement, the hypothesis may be put forth that the "failures" will have a reinforced motivation for retrenchment in the "private sphere."[16]

Another, peculiarly modern, articulation of the themes of self-expression and self-realization is sexuality. In view of the prominent place occupied by sexuality in the modern sacred cosmos, however, it deserves special consideration. The rigidity with which various aspects of sexual conduct are institutionalized in traditional societies attests to the difficulty in regulating such basic, and, in a sense, "private" conduct by external controls—as well as to the importance of such regulation for the kinship system. Wherever the kinship system is a central dimension of the social structure, pertinent norms are typically endowed with religious significance and are socially enforced. With specialization of the primary institutional domains, however, the family and, thus, sexuality lose some of their relevance for those domains and the enforcement of norms regulating the family and sexual conduct *becomes less important.* One may say, with some qualifications, that the family and sexuality recede more and more into the "private sphere." Conversely, to the extent that sexuality is "freed" from external social control, it becomes capable of assuming a crucial function in the "autonomous" individual's quest for self-expression and self-realization. This argument obviously does not imply that sexuality was unimportant or lacked urgency for men before the modern industrial period. Nor does it imply that sexuality did not have religious significance in the traditional sacred cosmos. It does imply, however, that sexuality, in connection with the "sacred" themes of self-expression and self-realization, now comes to play a unique role as a source of "ultimate" significance for the individual who is retrenched in the "private sphere." It is likely that the development which led from the notions of romantic love to what we may call, tongue-in-cheek, the sexual polytheism of the respectable suburbanite, represents more than a short-lived swing of the pendulum from which the weights of Victorian taboos were removed.

The far-reaching (although, of course, not complete) "liberation" of sexuality from social control permits sexual conduct to be governed more radically than in a traditional social order by consumer preference. It should be noted, however, that sexuality—while a basic component of individual "autonomy"—permits an enlargement of the "private sphere" beyond the solitary individual and, thus, may serve as a form of self-transcendence. At the same time, it is a form of self-transcendence which remains limited to the "private sphere" and is, one is tempted to say, innocuous from the point of view of a social order that is based, essentially, upon the functionally rational norms of the primary public institutions.

In the definition of the problem and in the description of the character of religion in modern society we adopted and tried to maintain an attitude of detachment. We hoped to avoid thereby the narrowing of perspectives that results so frequently in the analysis of religion not only from the various distinct forms of ideological bias but also from assumptions that are commonly taken for granted even in sociological theory. Where the analysis was supported directly by empirical evidence, it was necessary merely to exercise a certain amount of caution in generalizing from the data. Where the argumentation had to rely on indirect and scattered evidence, however, it was clearly impossible to refrain from using criteria of relevance which were derived from the implications of a theoretical position. In this case the temptation to over-interpret symptoms and to see connections which are merely plausible is indubitably great and we stress again the tentative character of some of the conclusions that were advanced. Nevertheless, we tried throughout to hold ourselves to the task at hand, to analyze rather than to evaluate. The question of how the profound changes in the character of religion in modern society affect individual existence, however, touches upon matters of personal concern to everyone. It may be permissible, at the end, to relax the neutrality to which we felt obligated during the previous discussion.

The discrepancy between the subjective "autonomy" of the individual in modern society and the objective autonomy of the primary institutional domains strikes us as critical. The primary social institutions have "emigrated" from the sacred cosmos. Their functional rationality is not part of a system that could be of "ultimate" significance to the individuals in the society. This removes from the primary institutions much of the (potentially intolerant) human pathos that proved to be fateful all too often in human history. If the process could be viewed in isolation it could justifiably appear as an essential component in freeing social arrangements from primitive emotions. The increasing autonomy of the primary public institutions, however, has consequences for the relation of the individual to the social order—and thus, ultimately, to himself. Reviewing some of these consequences one is equally justified in describing this process as a process of dehumanization of the basic structural components of the social order. The functional rationality of the primary social institutions seems to reinforce the isolation of the individual from his society, contributing thereby to the precariousness inherent in all social orders. Autonomy of the primary institutions, "subjective" autonomy and *anomie* of the social order are dialectically related. At the very least it may be said that "subjective" autonomy and autonomy of the primary institutions, the two most remarkable characteristics of modern industrial societies, are genuinely ambivalent phenomena.

The new social form of religion emerges in the same global transformation of society which leads to the autonomy of the primary public institutions. The modern sacred cosmos legitimates the retreat of the individual into the "private sphere" and sanctifies his subjective "autonomy." Thus it inevitably reinforces the autonomous functioning of the primary institutions. By bestowing a sacred quality upon the increasing subjectivity of human existence it supports not only the secularization but also what we called the dehumanization of the social structure. If this still appears paradoxical we have failed in driving home the point of this essay.

The modern sacred cosmos appears to operate as a *total* ideology. It provides an encompassing assortment of plausible ideas which supports the functioning of modern industrial societies—but *without* explicitly legitimating them. The final clause in the preceding sentence indicates one reason why it is not particularly useful to call the new social form of religion an ideology in the ordinary sense. In addition, the new social form of religion does *not* represent the vested interests of a particular social stratum and it is not articulated as a program of political and social action. It is neither utopian nor restorationist, neither communist nor capitalistic. It is doubtful whether the traditional social forms of religion can be adequately understood by attaching to them the label of ideology, notwithstanding their occasional ideological functions. The label would be indubitably misplaced in the case of the new social form of religion—for the reasons that were just mentioned.

How is one to decide whether the new social form of

religion is "good" or "bad"? It is a radically subjective form of "religiosity" that is characterized by a weakly coherent and nonobligatory sacred cosmos and by a low degree of "transcendence" in comparison to traditional modes of religion. Is this good or bad?

While the new social form of religion supports the de-humanization of the social structure, it also "sacralizes" the (relative) liberation of human *consciousness* from the constraint of the latter. This liberation represents a his-torically unprecedented opportunity for the autonomy of personal life for "everybody." It also contains a serious danger—of motivating mass withdrawal into the "private sphere" while "Rome burns." On balance, is this good or bad?

No matter how one answers this question, the effort to try to understand what is a revolutionary change in the relation of the individual to the social order can hardly be misspent. The emergence of the new social form of religion is partly obscured by the more easily visible economic and political characteristics of modern indus-trial society. It is unlikely that the trend we have tried to describe is reversible—even if such a reversal were con-sidered desirable. One must not avoid seeing it because one clings to traditionalist religious illusions. Nor must one ignore its implications because one may be inspired by secularist optimism.

V
ROBERT N. BELLAH

Civil Religion in America

WHILE SOME have argued that Christianity is the national faith, and others that church and synagogue celebrate only the generalized religion of "the American Way
of Life," few have realized that there actually exists alongside of and rather clearly differentiated from the churches
an elaborate and well-institutionalized civil religion in
America. This article argues not only that there is such
a thing, but also that this religion—or perhaps better, this
religious dimension—has its own seriousness and integrity
and requires the same care in understanding that any
other religion does.[1]

THE KENNEDY INAUGURAL

Kennedy's inaugural address of 20 January 1961 serves
as an example and a clue with which to introduce this
complex subject. That address began:

> We observe today not a victory of party but a celebration
> of freedom—symbolizing an end as well as a beginning—
> signifying renewal as well as change. For I have sworn be-
> fore you and almighty God the same solemn oath our fore-
> bears prescribed nearly a century and three quarters ago.
> The world is very different now. For man holds in his
> mortal hands the power to abolish all forms of human pov-
> erty and all forms of human life. And yet the same revolu-
> tionary beliefs for which our forebears fought are still at
> issue around the globe—the belief that the rights of man

From *Daedalus, Journal of the American Arts and Sciences,* Vol. 96,
No. 1. Reprinted by permission.

come not from the generosity of the state but from the hand of God.

And it concluded:

> Finally, whether you are citizens of America or citizens of the world, ask of us here the same high standards of strength and sacrifice which we ask of you. With a good conscience our only sure reward, with history the final judge of our deeds, let us go forth to lead the land we love, asking His blessing and His help, but knowing that here on earth God's work must truly be our own.

These are the three places in this brief address in which Kennedy mentioned the name of God. If we could understand why he mentioned God, the way in which he did it, and what he meant to say in those three references, we would understand much about American civil religion. But this is not a simple or obvious task, and American students of religion would probably differ widely in their interpretation of these passages.

Let us consider first the placing of the three references. They occur in the two opening paragraphs and in the closing paragraph, thus providing a sort of frame for the more concrete remarks that form the middle part of the speech. Looking beyond this particular speech, we would find that similar references to God are almost invariably to be found in the pronouncements of American presidents on solemn occasions, though usually not in the working messages that the president sends to Congress on various concrete issues. How, then, are we to interpret this placing of references to God?

It might be argued that the passages quoted reveal the essentially irrelevant role of religion in the very secular society that is America. The placing of the references in this speech as well as in public life generally indicates that religion has "only a ceremonial significance"; it gets only a sentimental nod which serves largely to placate the more unenlightened members of the community, before a discussion of the really serious business with which religion has nothing whatever to do. A cynical observer might even say that an American president has to mention God or risk losing votes. A semblance of piety is merely one of the unwritten qualifications for the office, a bit more traditional than but not essentially different from the present-day requirement of a pleasing television personality.

But we know enough about the function of ceremonial and ritual in various societies to make us suspicious of dismissing something as unimportant because it is "only a ritual." What people say on solemn occasions need not be taken at face value, but it is often indicative of deep-seated values and commitments that are not made explicit in the course of everyday life. Following this line of argument, it is worth considering whether the very special placing of the references to God in Kennedy's address may not reveal something rather important and serious about religion in American life.

It might be countered that the very way in which Kennedy made his reference reveals the essentially vestigial place of religion today. He did not refer to any religion in particular. He did not refer to Jesus Christ, or to Moses, or to the Christian church; certainly he did not refer to the Catholic Church. In fact, his only reference was to the concept of God, a word which almost all Americans can accept but which means so many different things to so many different people that it is almost an empty sign. Is this not just another indication that in America religion is considered vaguely to be a good thing, but that people care so little about it that it has lost any content whatever? Isn't Eisenhower reported to have said, "Our government makes no sense unless it is founded in a deeply felt religious faith—and I don't care what it is,"[2] and isn't that a complete negation of any real religion?

These questions are worth pursuing because they raise the issue of how civil religion relates to the political society, on the one hand, and to private religious organization, on the other. President Kennedy was a Christian, more specifically a Catholic Christian. Thus, his general references to God do not mean that he lacked a specific religious commitment. But why, then, did he not include some remark to the effect that Christ is the Lord of the world or some indication of respect for the Catholic Church? He did not because these are matters of his own private religious belief and of his relation to his own particular church; they are not matters relevant in any direct way to the conduct of his public office. Others with different religious views and commitments to different churches or denominations are equally qualified participants in the political process. The principle of separation of church and state guarantees the freedom of religious belief and association, but at the same time clearly segregates the religious sphere, which is considered to be essentially private, from the political one.

Considering the separation of church and state, how is a president justified in using the word "God" at all? The answer is that the separation of church and state has not denied the political realm a religious dimension. Although matters of personal religious belief, worship, and association are considered to be strictly private affairs, there are, at the same time, certain common elements of religious orientation that the great majority of Americans share. These have played a crucial role in the development of American institutions and still provide a religious dimension for the whole fabric of American life, including the political sphere. This public religious dimension is expressed in a set of beliefs, symbols, and rituals that I am calling the American civil religion. The inauguration of a president is an important ceremonial event in this religion. It reaffirms, among other things, the religious legitimation of the highest political authority.

Let us look more closely at what Kennedy actually said.

First he said, "I have sworn before you and Almighty God the same solemn oath our forebears prescribed nearly a century and three quarters ago." The oath is the oath of office, including the acceptance of the obligation to uphold the Constitution. He swears it before the people (you) and God. Beyond the Constitution, then, the president's obligation extends not only to the people but to God. In American political theory, sovereignty rests, of course, with the people, but implicitly, and often explicitly, the ultimate sovereignty has been attributed to God. This is the meaning of the motto "In God we trust," as well as the inclusion of the phrase "under God" in the pledge to the flag. What difference does it make that sovereignty belongs to God? Though the will of the people as expressed in majority vote is carefully institutionalized as the operative source of political authority, it is deprived of an ultimate significance. The will of the people is not itself the criterion of right and wrong. There is a higher criterion in terms of which this will can be judged; it is possible that the people may be wrong. The president's obligation extends to the higher criterion.

When Kennedy says that "the rights of man come not from the generosity of the state but from the hand of God," he is stressing this point again. It does not matter whether the state is the expression of the will of an autocratic monarch or of the "people"; the rights of man are more basic than any political structure and provide a point of revolutionary leverage from which any state structure may be radically altered. That is the basis for his reassertion of the revolutionary significance of America.

But the religious dimension in political life as recognized by Kennedy not only provides a grounding for the rights of man which makes any form of political absolutism illegitimate, it also provides a transcendent goal for the political process. This is implied in his final words that "here on earth God's work must truly be our own."

What he means here is, I think, more clearly spelled out in a previous paragraph, the wording of which, incidentally, has a distinctly Biblical ring:

> Now the trumpet summons us again—not as a call to bear arms, though arms we need—not as a call to battle, though embattled we are—but a call to bear the burden of a long twilight struggle, year in and year out, "rejoicing in hope, patient in tribulation"—a struggle against the common enemies of man: tyranny, poverty, disease and war itself.

The whole address can be understood as only the most recent statement of a theme that lies very deep in the American tradition, namely the obligation, both collective and individual, to carry out God's will on earth. This was the motivating spirit of those who founded America, and it has been present in every generation since. Just below the surface throughout Kennedy's inaugural address, it becomes explicit in the closing statement that God's work must be our own. That this very activist and noncontemplative conception of the fundamental religious obligation, which has been historically associated with the Protestant position, should be enunciated so clearly in the first major statement of the first Catholic president seems to underline how deeply established it is in the American outlook. Let us now consider the form and history of the civil religious tradition in which Kennedy was speaking.

The Idea of a Civil Religion

The phrase "civil religion" is, of course, Rousseau's. In Chapter 8, Book 4, of *The Social Contract,* he outlines the simple dogmas of the civil religion: the existence of God, the life to come, the reward of virtue and the punishment of vice, and the exclusion of religious intolerance. All other religious opinions are outside the cognizance of the state and may be freely held by citizens. While the phrase "civil religion" was not used, to the best of my knowledge, by the founding fathers, and I am certainly not arguing for the particular influence of Rousseau, it is clear that similar ideas, as part of the cultural climate of the late-eighteenth century, were to be found among the Americans. For example, Franklin writes in his autobiography:

I never was without some religious principles. I never doubted, for instance, the existence of the Deity; that he made the world and govern'd it by his Providence; that the most acceptable service of God was the doing of good to men; that our souls are immortal; and that all crime will be punished, and virtue rewarded either here or hereafter. These I esteemed the essentials of every religion; and, being to be found in all the religions we had in our country, I respected them all, tho' with different degrees of respect, as I found them more or less mix'd with other articles, which, without any tendency to inspire, promote or confirm morality, serv'd principally to divide us, and make us unfriendly to one another.

It is easy to dispose of this sort of position as essentially utilitarian in relation to religion. In Washington's Farewell Address (though the words may be Hamilton's) the utilitarian aspect is quite explicit:

Of all the dispositions and habits which lead to political prosperity, Religion and Morality are indispensable supports. In vain would that man claim the tribute of Patriotism, who should labour to subvert these great Pillars of human happiness, these firmest props of the duties of men and citizens. The mere politician, equally with the pious man ought to respect and cherish them. A volume could not trace all their connections with private and public felicity. Let it simply be asked where is the security for property, for reputation, for life, if the sense of religious obligation *desert* the oaths, which are the instruments of investigation in Courts of Justice? And let us with caution indulge the supposition, that morality can be maintained without religion. Whatever may be conceded to the influence of refined education on minds of peculiar structure, reason and expe-

rience both forbid us to expect that National morality can
prevail in exclusion of religious principle.

But there is every reason to believe that religion, particularly the idea of God, played a constitutive role in the
thought of the early American statesmen.

Kennedy's inaugural pointed to the religious aspect of
the Declaration of Independence, and it might be well to
look at that document a bit more closely. There are four
references to God. The first speaks of the "Laws of Nature
and of Nature's God" which entitle any people to be independent. The second is the famous statement that all men
"are endowed by their Creator with certain inalienable
Rights." Here Jefferson is locating the fundamental legitimacy of the new nation in a conception of "higher law"
that is itself based on both classical natural law and Biblical religion. The third is an appeal to "the Supreme
Judge of the world for the rectitude of our intentions,"
and the last indicates "a firm reliance on the protection
of divine Providence." In these last two references, a
Biblical God of history who stands in judgment over the
world is indicated.

The intimate relation of these religious notions with the
self-conception of the new republic is indicated by the
frequency of their appearance in early official documents.
For example, we find in Washington's first inaugural
address of 30 April 1789:

> It would be peculiarly improper to omit in this first of-
> ficial act my fervent supplications to that Almighty Being
> who rules over the universe, who presides in the councils
> of nations, and whose providential aids can supply every
> defect, that His benediction may consecrate to the liberties
> and happiness of the people of the United States a Govern-
> ment instituted by themselves for these essential purposes,
> and may enable every instrument employed in its ad-
> ministration to execute with success the functions allotted
> to his charge.
> No people can be bound to acknowledge and adore the

Invisible Hand which conducts the affairs of man more than those of the United States. Every step by which we have advanced to the character of an independent nation seems to have been distinguished by some token of providential agency. . . .

The propitious smiles of Heaven can never be expected on a nation that disregards the eternal rules of order and right which Heaven itself has ordained. . . . The preservation of the sacred fire of liberty and the destiny of the republican model of government are justly considered, perhaps, as *deeply*, as *finally*, staked on the experiment intrusted to the hands of the American people.

Nor did these religious sentiments remain merely the personal expression of the president. At the request of both Houses of Congress, Washington proclaimed on October 3 of that same first year as president that November 26 should be "a day of public thanksgiving and prayer," the first Thanksgiving Day under the Constitution.

The words and acts of the founding fathers, especially the first few presidents, shaped the form and tone of the civil religion as it has been maintained ever since. Though much is selectively derived from Christianity, this religion is clearly not itself Christianity. For one thing, neither Washington nor Adams nor Jefferson mentions Christ in his inaugural address; nor do any of the subsequent presidents, although not one of them fails to mention God.[3] The God of the civil religion is not only rather "unitarian," he is also on the austere side, much more related to order, law, and right than to salvation and love. Even though he is somewhat deist in cast, he is by no means simply a watchmaker God. He is actively interested and involved in history, with a special concern for America. Here the analogy has much less to do with natural law than with ancient Israel; the equation of America with Israel in the idea of the "American Israel" is not infrequent.[4] What was implicit in the words of Washington already quoted becomes explicit in Jefferson's second inaugural when he said: "I shall need, too, the favor of that Being in whose hands we are, who led our fathers, as Israel of old, from their native land and planted them in a country flowing with all the necessaries and comforts of life." Europe is Egypt; America, the promised land. God has led his people to establish a new sort of social order that shall be a light unto all the nations.[5]

This theme, too, has been a continuous one in the civil religion. We have already alluded to it in the case of the Kennedy inaugural. We find it again in President Johnson's inaugural address:

> They came here—the exile and the stranger, brave but frightened—to find a place where a man could be his own man. They made a covenant with this land. Conceived in justice, written in liberty, bound in union, it was meant one day to inspire the hopes of all mankind; and it binds us still. If we keep its terms, we shall flourish.

What we have, then, from the earliest years of the republic is a collection of beliefs, symbols, and rituals with respect to sacred things and institutionalized in a collectivity. This religion—there seems no other word for it—while not antithetical to and indeed sharing much in common with Christianity, was neither sectarian nor in any specific sense Christian. At a time when the society was overwhelmingly Christian, it seems unlikely that this lack of Christian reference was meant to spare the feelings of the tiny non-Christian minority. Rather, the civil religion expressed what those who set the precedents felt was appropriate under the circumstances. It reflected their private as well as public views. Nor was the civil religion simply "religion in general." While generality was undoubtedly seen as a virtue by some, as in the quotation from Franklin above, the civil religion was specific enough when it came to the topic of America. Precisely because of this specificity, the civil religion was saved from empty formalism and served as a genuine vehicle of national religious self-understanding.

But the civil religion was not, in the minds of Franklin, Washington, Jefferson, or other leaders, with the exception of a few radicals like Tom Paine, ever felt to be a substitute for Christianity. There was an implicit but quite clear division of function between the civil religion and Christianity. Under the doctrine of religious liberty, an exceptionally wide sphere of personal piety and voluntary social action was left to the churches. But the churches were neither to control the state nor to be controlled by it. The national magistrate, whatever his private religious views, operates under the rubrics of the civil religion as long as he is in his official capacity, as we have already seen in the case of Kennedy. This accommodation was undoubtedly the product of a particular historical moment and of a cultural background dominated by Protestantism of several varieties and the Enlightenment, but it has survived despite subsequent changes in the cultural and religious climate.

CIVIL WAR AND CIVIL RELIGION

Until the Civil War, the American civil religion focused above all on the event of the Revolution, which was seen as the final act of the exodus from the old lands across the waters. The Declaration of Independence and the Constitution were the sacred scriptures and Washington the divinely appointed Moses who led his people out of the hands of tyranny. The Civil War, which Sidney Mead calls "the center of American history,"[6] was the second great event that involved the national self-understanding so deeply as to require expression in the civil religion. In 1835, Tocqueville wrote that the American republic had never really been tried, that victory in the Revolutionary War was more the result of British preoccupation elsewhere and the presence of a powerful ally than of any great military success of the Americans. But in 1861 the time of testing had indeed come. Not only did the Civil War have the tragic intensity of fratricidal strife, but it was one of the bloodiest wars of the nineteenth century; the loss of life was far greater than any previously suffered by Americans.

The Civil War raised the deepest questions of national meaning. The man who not only formulated but in his own person embodied its meaning for Americans was Abraham Lincoln. For him the issue was not in the first instance slavery but "whether that nation, or any nation so conceived, and so dedicated, can long endure." He had said in Independence Hall in Philadelphia on 22 February 1861:

> All the political sentiments I entertain have been drawn, so far as I have been able to draw them, from the sentiments which originated in and were given to the world from this Hall. I have never had a feeling, politically, that did not spring from the sentiments embodied in the Declaration of Independence.[7]

The phrases of Jefferson constantly echo in Lincoln's speeches. His task was, first of all, to save the Union—not for America alone but for the meaning of America to the whole world so unforgettably etched in the last phrase of the Gettysburg Address.

But inevitably the issue of slavery as the deeper cause of the conflict had to be faced. In the second inaugural, Lincoln related slavery and the war in an ultimate perspective:

> If we shall suppose that American slavery is one of those offenses which, in the providence of God, must needs come, but which, having continued through His appointed time, He now wills to remove, and that He gives to both North and South this terrible war as the woe due to those by whom the offense came, shall we discern therein any departure from those divine attributes which the believers in

a living God always ascribe to Him? Fondly do we hope, fervently do we pray, that this mighty scourge of war may speedily pass away. Yet, if God wills that it continue until all the wealth piled by the bondsman's two hundred and fifty years of unrequited toil shall be sunk, and until every drop of blood drawn with the lash shall be paid by another drawn with the sword, as was said three thousand years ago, so still it must be said "the judgements of the Lord are true and righteous altogether."

But he closes on a note if not of redemption then of reconciliation—"With malice toward none, with charity for all. . . ."

With the Civil War, a new theme of death, sacrifice, and rebirth enters the civil religion. It is symbolized in the life and death of Lincoln. Nowhere is it stated more vividly than in the Gettysburg Address, itself part of the Lincolnian "New Testament" among the civil scriptures. Robert Lowell has recently pointed out the "insistent use of birth images" in this speech explicitly devoted to "these honored dead": "brought forth," "conceived," "created," "a new birth of freedom." He goes on to say:

> The Gettysburg Address is a symbolic and sacramental act. Its verbal quality is resonance combined with a logical, matter of fact, prosaic brevity. . . . In his words, Lincoln symbolically died, just as the Union soldiers really died— and as he himself was soon really to die. By his words, he gave the field of battle a symbolic significance that it had lacked. For us and our country, he left Jefferson's ideals of freedom and equality joined to the Christian sacrificial act of death and rebirth. I believe this is a meaning that goes beyond sect or religion and beyond peace and war, and is now part of our lives as a challenge, obstacle and hope.[8]

Lowell is certainly right in pointing out the Christian quality of the symbolism here, but he is also right in quickly disavowing any sectarian implication. The earlier symbolism of the civil religion had been Hebraic without being in any sense Jewish. The Gettysburg symbolism

("... those who here gave their lives, that that nation might live") is Christian without having anything to do with the Christian church.

The symbolic equation of Lincoln with Jesus was made relatively early. Herndon, who had been Lincoln's law partner, wrote:

> For fifty years God rolled Abraham Lincoln through his fiery furnace. He did it to try Abraham and to purify him for his purposes. This made Mr. Lincoln humble, tender, forbearing, sympathetic to suffering, kind, sensitive, tolerant; broadening, deepening and widening his whole nature; making him the noblest and loveliest character since Jesus Christ. ... I believe that Lincoln was God's chosen one.[9]

With the Christian archetype in the background, Lincoln, "our martyred president," was linked to the war dead, those who "gave the last full measure of devotion." The theme of sacrifice was indelibly written into the civil religion.

The new symbolism soon found both physical and ritualistic expression. The great number of the war dead required the establishment of a number of national cemeteries. Of these, the Gettysburg National Cemetery, which Lincoln's famous address served to dedicate, has been overshadowed only by the Arlington National Cemetery. Begun somewhat vindictively on the Lee estate across the river from Washington, partly with the end that the Lee family could never reclaim it,[10] it has subsequently become the most hallowed monument of the civil religion. Not only was a section set aside for the Confederate dead, but it has received the dead of each succeeding American war. It is the site of the one important new symbol to come out of World War I, the Tomb of the Unknown Soldier; more recently it has become the site of the tomb of another martyred president and its symbolic eternal flame.

Memorial Day, which grew out of the Civil War, gave ritual expression to the themes we have been discussing. As Lloyd Warner has so brilliantly analyzed it, the Memorial Day observance, especially in the towns and smaller cities of America, is a major event for the whole community, involving a rededication to the martyred dead, to the spirit of sacrifice, and to the American vision.[11] Just as Thanksgiving Day, which incidentally was securely institutionalized as an annual national holiday only under the presidency of Lincoln, serves to integrate the family into the civil religion, so Memorial Day has acted to integrate the local community into the national cult. Together with the less overtly religious Fourth of July and the more minor celebrations of Veterans Day and the birthdays of Washington and Lincoln, these two holidays provide an annual ritual calendar for the civil religion. The public school system serves as a particularly important context for the cultic celebration of the civil rituals.

THE CIVIL RELIGION TODAY

In reifying and giving a name to something that, though pervasive enough when you look at it, has gone on only semiconsciously, there is risk of severely distorting the data. But the reification and the naming have already begun. The religious critics of "religion in general," or of the "religion of the 'American Way of Life,'" or of "American Shinto" have really been talking about the civil religion. As usual in religious polemic, they take as criteria the best in their own religious tradition and as typical the worst in the tradition of the civil religion. Against these critics, I would argue that the civil religion at its best is a genuine apprehension of universal and transcendent religious reality as seen in or, one could almost say, as revealed through the experience of the American people. Like all religions, it has suffered various deformations and demonic distortions. At its best, it has neither been so general that it has lacked incisive relevance to the American scene nor so particular that it has placed American society above universal human values. I am not at all convinced that the leaders of the churches have consistently represented a higher level of religious insight than the spokesmen of the civil religion. Reinhold Niebuhr has this to say of Lincoln, who never joined a church and who certainly represents civil religion at its best:

> An analysis of the religion of Abraham Lincoln in the context of the traditional religion of his time and place and of its polemical use on the slavery issue, which corrupted religious life in the days before and during the Civil War, must lead to the conclusion that Lincoln's religious convictions were superior in depth and purity to those, not only of the political leaders of his day, but of the religious leaders of the era.[12]

Perhaps the real animus of the religious critics has been not so much against the civil religion in itself but against its pervasive and dominating influence within the sphere of church religion. As S. M. Lipset has recently shown, American religion at least since the early-nineteenth century has been predominantly activist, moralistic, and social rather than contemplative, theological, or innerly spiritual.[13] Tocqueville spoke of American church religion as "a political institution which powerfully contributes to the maintenance of a democratic republic among the Americans"[14] by supplying a strong moral consensus amidst continuous political change. Henry Bargy in 1902 spoke of American church religion as *"la poésie du civisme."*[15]

It is certainly true that the relation between religion and politics in America has been singularly smooth. This is in large part due to the dominant tradition. As Tocqueville wrote:

> The greatest part of British America was peopled by men who, after having shaken off the authority of the Pope, acknowledged no other religious supremacy: they brought with them into the New World a form of Christianity which I cannot better describe than by styling it a democratic and republican religion.[16]

The churches opposed neither the Revolution nor the establishment of democratic institutions. Even when some of them opposed the full institutionalization of religious liberty, they accepted the final outcome with good grace and without nostalgia for an *ancien régime*. The American civil religion was never anticlerical or militantly secular. On the contrary, it borrowed selectively from the religious tradition in such a way that the average American saw no conflict between the two. In this way, the civil religion was able to build up without any bitter struggle with the church powerful symbols of national solidarity and to mobilize deep levels of personal motivation for the attainment of national goals.

Such an achievement is by no means to be taken for granted. It would seem that the problem of a civil religion is quite general in modern societies and that the way it is solved or not solved will have repercussions in many spheres. One needs only to think of France to see how differently things can go. The French Revolution was anticlerical to the core and attempted to set up an antichristian civil religion. Throughout modern French history, the chasm between traditional Catholic symbols and the symbolism of 1789 has been immense.

American civil religion is still very much alive. Just three years ago we participated in a vivid reenactment of the sacrifice theme in connection with the funeral of our assassinated president. The American Israel theme is clearly behind both Kennedy's New Frontier and Johnson's Great Society. Let me give just one recent illustration of how the civil religion serves to mobilize support for the attainment of national goals. On 15 March 1965 President Johnson went before Congress to ask for a strong voting-rights bill. Early in the speech he said:

> Rarely are we met with the challenge, not to our growth or abundance, or our welfare or our security—but rather to the values and the purposes and the meaning of our beloved nation.
>
> The issue of equal rights for American Negroes is such an issue. And should we defeat every enemy, and should we double our wealth and conquer the stars and still be unequal to this issue, then we will have failed as a people and as a nation.
>
> For with a country as with a person, "What is a man profited, if he shall gain the whole world, and lose his own soul?"

And in conclusion he said:

> Above the pyramid on the great seal of the United States it says in Latin, "God has favored our undertaking."
>
> God will not favor everything that we do. It is rather our duty to divine his will. I cannot help but believe that He truly understands and that He really favors the undertaking that we begin here tonight.[17]

The civil religion has not always been invoked in favor of worthy causes. On the domestic scene, an American-Legion type of ideology that fuses God, country, and flag has been used to attack nonconformist and liberal ideas and groups of all kinds. Still, it has been difficult to use the words of Jefferson and Lincoln to support special interests and undermine personal freedom. The defenders of slavery before the Civil War came to reject the thinking of the Declaration of Independence. Some of the most consistent of them turned against not only Jeffersonian democracy but Reformation religion; they dreamed of a South dominated by medieval chivalry and divine-right monarchy.[18] For all the overt religiosity of the radical right today, their relation to the civil religious consensus is tenuous, as when the John Birch Society attacks the central American symbol of Democracy itself.

With respect to America's role in the world, the dangers of distortion are greater and the built-in safeguards of the tradition weaker. The theme of the American Israel was used, almost from the beginning, as a justification for the shameful treatment of the Indians so characteristic of our history. It can be overtly or implicitly linked to the idea of manifest destiny which has been used to legitimate several adventures in imperialism since the early-nineteenth century. Never has the danger been greater than today. The issue is not so much one of imperial expansion, of which we are accused, as of the tendency to assimilate all governments or parties in the world which support our immediate policies or call upon our help by invoking the notion of free institutions and democratic values. Those nations that are for the moment "on our side" become "the free world." A repressive and unstable military dictatorship in South Vietnam becomes "the free people of South Vietnam and their government."

It is then part of the role of America as the New Jerusalem and "the last best hope of earth" to defend such governments with treasure and eventually with blood. When our soldiers are actually dying, it becomes possible to consecrate the struggle further by invoking the great theme of sacrifice. For the majority of the American people who are unable to judge whether the people in South Vietnam (or wherever) are "free like us," such arguments are convincing. Fortunately President Johnson has been less ready to assert that "God has favored our undertaking" in the case of Vietnam than with respect to civil rights. But others are not so hesitant. The civil religion has exercised long-term pressure for the humane solution of our greatest domestic problem, the treatment of the Negro American. It remains to be seen how relevant it can become for our role in the world at large, and whether we can effectually stand for "the revolutionary beliefs for which our forebears fought," in John F. Kennedy's words.

The civil religion is obviously involved in the most pressing moral and political issues of the day. But it is also caught in another kind of crisis, theoretical and theological, of which it is at the moment largely unaware. "God" has clearly been a central symbol in the civil religion from the beginning and remains so today. This symbol is just as central to the civil religion as it is to Judaism or Christianity. In the late-eighteenth century this posed no problem; even Tom Paine, contrary to his detractors, was not an atheist. From left to right and regardless of church or sect, all could accept the idea of God. But today, as even *Time* has recognized, the meaning of the word "God" is by no means so clear or so obvious. There is no formal creed in the civil religion. We have had a Catholic president; it is conceivable that we could have a Jewish one. But could we have an agnostic president? Could a man with conscientious scruples about using the word "God" the way Kennedy and Johnson have used it be elected chief magistrate of our country? If the whole God symbolism requires reformulation, there will be obvious consequences for the civil religion, consequences perhaps of liberal alienation and of fundamentalist ossification that have not so far been prominent in this realm. The civil religion has been a point of articulation between the profoundest commitments of the Western religious and philosophical tradition and the common beliefs of ordinary Americans. It is not too soon to consider how the deepening theological crisis may affect the future of this articulation.

The Third Time of Trial

In conclusion it may be worthwhile to relate the civil religion to the most serious situation that we as Americans now face, what I call the third time of trial. The first time of trial had to do with the question of independence, whether we should or could run our own affairs in our own way. The second time of trial was over the issue of slavery, which in turn was only the most salient aspect of the more general problem of the full institutionalization of democracy within our country. This second problem we are still far from solving though we have some notable successes to our credit. But we have been overtaken by a third great problem which has led to a third great crisis, in the midst of which we stand. This is the problem of responsible action in a revolutionary world, a world seeking to attain many of the things, material and spiritual, that we have already attained. Americans have, from the beginning, been aware of the responsibility and the significance our republican experiment has for the whole world. The first internal political polarization in the new nation had to do with our attitude toward the French Revolution. But we were small and weak then, and "foreign entanglements" seemed to threaten our very survival. During the last century, our relevance for the world was not forgotten, but our role was seen as purely exemplary. Our democratic republic rebuked tyranny by merely existing. Just after World War I we were on the brink of taking a different role in the world, but once again we turned our back.

Since World War II the old pattern has become impossible. Every president since Roosevelt has been groping toward a new pattern of action in the world, one that would be consonant with our power and our responsibilities. For Truman and for the period dominated by John Foster Dulles that pattern was seen to be the great Manichaean confrontation of East and West, the confrontation of democracy and "the false philosophy of Communism" that provided the structure of Truman's inaugural address. But with the last years of Eisenhower and with the successive two presidents, the pattern began to shift. The great problems came to be seen as caused not solely by the evil intent of any one group of men, but as stemming from much more complex and multiple sources. For Kennedy, it was not so much a struggle against particular men as against "the common enemies of man: tyranny, poverty, disease and war itself."

But in the midst of this trend toward a less primitive conception of ourselves and our world, we have somehow, without anyone really intending it, stumbled into a military confrontation where we have come to feel that our honor is at stake. We have in a moment of uncertainty been tempted to rely on our overwhelming physical power rather than on our intelligence, and we have, in part, succumbed to this temptation. Bewildered and unnerved when our terrible power fails to bring immediate success, we are at the edge of a chasm the depth of which no man knows.

I cannot help but think of Robinson Jeffers, whose poetry seems more apt now than when it was written, when he said:

> Unhappy country, what wings you have! . . .
> Weep (it is frequent in human affairs), weep
>   for the terrible magnificence of the means,
> The ridiculous incompetence of the reasons,
>   the bloody and shabby
> Pathos of the result.

But as so often before in similar times, we have a man of prophetic stature, without the bitterness or misanthropy of Jeffers, who, as Lincoln before him, calls this nation to its judgment:

> When a nation is very powerful but lacking in self-confidence, it is likely to behave in a manner that is dangerous both to itself and to others.
> Gradually but unmistakably, America is succumbing to that arrogance of power which has afflicted, weakened and in some cases destroyed great nations in the past.
> If the war goes on and expands, if that fatal process con-

tinues to accelerate until America becomes what it is not now and never has been, a seeker after unlimited power and empire, then Vietnam will have had a mighty and tragic fallout indeed.

I do not believe that will happen. I am very apprehensive but I still remain hopeful, and even confident, that America, with its humane and democratic traditions, will find the wisdom to match its power.[19]

Without an awareness that our nation stands under higher judgment, the tradition of the civil religion would be dangerous indeed. Fortunately, the prophetic voices have never been lacking. Our present situation brings to mind the Mexican-American war that Lincoln, among so many others, opposed. The spirit of civil disobedience that is alive today in the civil rights movement and the opposition to the Vietnam war was already clearly outlined by Henry David Thoreau when he wrote, "If the law is of such a nature that it requires you to be an agent of injustice to another, then I say, break the law." Thoreau's words, "I would remind my countrymen that they are men first, and Americans at a late and convenient hour,"[20] provides an essential standard for any adequate thought and action in our third time of trial. As Americans, we have been well favored in the world, but it is as men that we will be judged.

Out of the first and second times of trial have come, as we have seen, the major symbols of the American civil religion. There seems little doubt that a successful negotiation of this third time of trial—the attainment of some kind of viable and coherent world order—would precipitate a major new set of symbolic forms. So far the flickering flame of the United Nations burns too low to be the focus of a cult, but the emergence of a genuine transnational sovereignty would certainly change this. It would necessitate the incorporation of vital international symbolism into our civil religion, or, perhaps a better way of putting it, it would result in American civil religion becoming simply one part of a new civil religion of the world. It is useless to speculate on the form such a civil religion might take, though it obviously would draw on religious traditions beyond the sphere of Biblical religion alone. Fortunately, since the American civil religion is not the worship of the American nation but an understanding of the American experience in the light of ultimate and universal reality, the reorganization entailed by such a new situation need not disrupt the American civil religion's continuity. A world civil religion could be accepted as a fulfillment and not a denial of American civil religion. Indeed, such an outcome has been the eschatological hope of American civil religion from the beginning. To deny such an outcome would be to deny the meaning of America itself.

Behind the civil religion at every point lie Biblical archetypes: exodus, chosen people, Promised Land, New Jerusalem, sacrificial death, and rebirth. But it is also genuinely American and genuinely new. It has its own prophets and its own martyrs, its own sacred events and sacred places, its own solemn rituals and symbols. It is concerned that America be a society as perfectly in accord with the will of God as men can make it, and a light to all the nations.

It has often been used and is being used today as a cloak for petty interests and ugly passions. It is in need —as is any living faith—of continual reformation, of being measured by universal standards. But it is not evident that it is incapable of growth and new insight.

It does not make any decision for us. It does not remove us from moral ambiguity, from being, in Lincoln's fine phrase, an "almost chosen people." But it is a heritage of moral and religious experience from which we still have much to learn as we formulate the decisions that lie ahead.

VI

CHARLES C. WEST

Community —
Christian and Secular

WHAT IS THE BASIS of human community? This question is not raised by people who are secure in their stable cultures and philosophies. Ideologists out to transform the world into the image of their ideal put it only as a foil for a certain answer. But the characteristic of our time is that this question is being asked by secular and religious men, by politicians, scientists, and philosophers in every part of the world, in a tone which shows that none feels that he knows the answer.

Ancient cultures are seeking in their national independence a self-identity they once thought they had. Ideological movements (notably communism, but also the humanist secularism of the western world) find that the social realities with which they must cope call their basic assumptions more and more in question. Religions of all kinds are being forced by events into that self-questioning which Jews and Christians have faced from the beginning because of the God they serve. The behavioral sciences underline the experience of all of us that the very communities in which our being takes shape —family, neighborhood, parish, class—are shifting, relative units made and broken by larger social forces, not structures of a permanent order. Communities, cultures, and ideologies, even where we cling to them or try to make them anew, are no longer the source of our cer-

From *Man in Community,* ed. by Egbert de Vries (Association Press, 1966). Copyright © 1966 by World Council of Churches. Reprinted by permission of World Council of Churches.

tainty and security. They have become tasks in an uncertain world.

This process, and our recognition of it, we know as secularization. It moves toward a state of human relations in which no religion or ideology dominates, and where no common sense of the timeless order of reality prevails. Is this a real possibility for modern man? Does this condition inevitably give rise to a flight toward religion, or a philosophy of secularism which imposes a humanist world view and an unlimited confidence in man on the world? Is it possible for man to live with the relativity which a fully secular society brings with it?

This writer believes in this possibility. He does so because he is a Christian and finds the secular attitude to be required by a faithful response to God's revelation in history. But he hopes to demonstrate also to non-Christians that secularization is not the practice of self-deception by unstable men and cultures, but the real state of affairs in society today, a state which is full both of dangers and promises for the future, and within which our responsibility for our fellow human beings is given to us.

SECULARIZATION

An earlier ecumenical study has defined this process as "the withdrawal of areas of life and thought from religious—and finally also from metaphysical—control, and the attempt to understand and live in these areas in the terms which they alone offer."[1] Such a definition has the advantage of coupling religious and secular world views and defining secularization as a movement away from both. But it hardly catches the drama which the word "life" implies, as familiar certainties are blotted out in the hurricane of events which has blown up in the last generation. It is the human crisis which concerns us mainly here. Let us look at it more closely.

1. Secularization is a process whereby men and societies have lost the sense of living in a totally coherent world the basic elements of which can be grasped by the human mind or by religious beliefs and practices. The word "empirical" suggests itself to describe this attitude, but it is deceptive. The spoiling of a beautiful theory by a single recalcitrant fact does not describe the way in which scientific investigation operates. Rather, it is in the realm of theory itself that total coherence has been lost. In the field of physics this has been dramatically illustrated by the disappearance of the mechanical model of the universe in favor of mathematical formulas of which no model can be made. But it is equally the case in economics, where the integrated theories which once undergirded capitalism or predicted its destruction have been replaced by a variety of functional models; in sociology, and not least in politics, where the great ideologies which at the end of the Second World War competed for the task of rebuilding the world have one and all lost their power to convince even the people under their influence of the power and truth of their basic ideas. Doubt about a coherent world has eroded not only religious institutions, but Communist, Social Democratic, and Christian Democratic parties, labor movements, patriotic associations, and countless other movements as well.

2. This in itself could be a healthy reaction, a return to concrete human realities from the abstractions which have bedeviled them. But beneath it lies a crisis, the crisis of being itself. Secularization is the process whereby men and societies have learned, more sharply than ever before, the relativity of human knowledge and ethics to the standpoint of the knower and the conditions of his investigation, or the character of his action. This was the insight of Hegel and Marx, though it goes back to David Hume. The world is known only by interaction with a collective or individual agent; and the resulting knowledge, or

value, is never detachable from that relation. Once again physics offers the most dramatic illustration: as the objective reality of physical substance dissolves in sometimes contradictory pictures (the wave and quantum theories of light) and the experimenter finds it less and less possible to discover that which the conditions of his experiment themselves do not help to create, the physicist magnifies human control over an unknowable reality to frightening and exhilarating proportions. The ontology of physics becomes ever more problematical; its functionality increases every day. So also with social existence. Ancient structures of the common life, cultural, economic, political, and familial in one, often rooted in a profound and ageless sense of relation to divinity, suddenly lose their power to give security and meaning to human community. As industry moves in, trade moves more rapidly and persons are forced to work, often alone, with those of other cultures, the ontological question loses its relevance also in the social sphere, and the question of function takes its place. Nature and society alike become, in the words of Guardini, "a complex interaction of relations and functions which can only be grasped by mathematical symbols, and which are based on something which can no longer be given a name."[2] Secularization is the experience—the critical experience—of losing contact with being, of no longer being able to grasp the structure of reality as it is in itself, and at the same time being caught up in a changing network of relations and functions wherein lies greater power for good and evil than was dreamed of by our ancestors.

3. Secularization involves, as a by-product of this functional direction, a movement toward specialization, in thought and life. By a curious paradox the organ of universalism in man's spirit—his ideology and religion, his sense of continuity with the being of all things—has been rendered obsolete by the reality of universal history into which mankind has been swept. It is demanded of mod-

ern man not that he explore some realm of being but that he master a field which has a functional value. The language of this field is related to its functionality; the psychologist, the sociologist, the physiologist, and the neurologist all study some function of man, but none feels it necessary to have a doctrine of man as a whole. Functional collaboration among them may be wise at times, but no overall theory need embrace them. But what works well in the realm of thought becomes a crisis for human existence. For secularized man is himself a bundle of specializations—that of his place of work, of his family life, of his circle of friends, and perhaps of his church or other group which claims a portion of his loyalty and time. The relevant confrontations with reality other than himself take place in these local, particular contexts, in the persons and conditions he meets there.

4. Secularized man, then, is integrated not by the structures of the world in which he lives but—if at all—by his sense of what it means to be a person in this network of relationship, and what it means to be responsible for the function and the power which lie in his hands. His is a terrifying freedom from which there is no escape in shifting the burden of his responsibility into some god or nation or philosophy of nature and history. As a nuclear physicist or a biochemist, he cannot beguile himself with confidence in the inevitable beneficence of scientific discoveries for man. As an industrialist amid automation he cannot escape with theories of economic progress his responsibility for the growing mass of unemployed semi-skilled workers which his policies help produce. As an African politician he cannot draw comfort in private from his public ideology of a developing nation catching up with Europe and America. As an American politician he becomes dangerous to his country and the world when he sincerely believes in "total victory" over the enemies of his way of life.

The list could be extended indefinitely. Responsibility

for the control of the power he himself has produced, for the fateful consequences of his own accomplishments in a world where metaphysical dreams no longer convince and where no superior power makes things right, is the hallmark of secularized man.

This is a dangerous and exposed position. Many of the greatest thinkers of our time regard it as an unstable one, a stage in the dramatic process of social decay which seeks to exclude the divine structure of reality which gave it birth only to end by setting up sacred absolutes of its own which are all the more rigid for being unrecognized as such. Mircea Eliade speaks of "raw religion," that urge to divinize portions of the world that is present in every man and culture. Paul Tillich speaks optimistically of extreme autonomy of man preparing the way for a new breakthrough of theonomy. But Roger Mehl describes the trend more ominously:

> We discover in the midst of secularized society a process of resacralization. Some turn back to the church as a sacred structure, some turn to secular religions. . . . They make no clear distinction between the sacred and the profane. They bring the sacred down to earth in a false incarnation which results in a self-deification of man.[3]

The flight to secular religion is furthermore only one of the dangers which beset us in this condition. Nihilism in its various forms threatens equally from the other side. Technology can become an end in itself for those fascinated by its processes, regardless of its human effects. The Sophists of ancient Greece who sold the art of argument to the highest bidder have their counterparts today in the physicists, chemists, biologists, and engineers who limit their horizon by the project in which they are engaged; in the economists and financiers whose ideas or policies are at the disposal of the particular interest that hires them; and in the technicians of politics and of advertising who manipulate the human mind for their clients. Power can be its own rationale in a world where "realists" reckon with no universal power which limits and judges their own. Human beings can be misused and their humanness destroyed not only by fanatic idealists, but also by cynics who recognize no objective values in society or structure to human nature. If Orwell's *1984* symbolizes the one type, Skinner's *Walden II* might stand for the other.

This is the demonology of secularization. But there remains one descriptive word to be said. Man without religion and metaphysics, man the problem solver alone with his responsibility for a world which he has made, remains a human being. There is implicit in the secular attitude an open reciprocal relation of man with man in the pursuit of truth and the solution of problems. There is an acceptance of the relativity of every man's point of view and interest and therefore of the inevitability of conflict and compromise. There is a search for the form of humanity not in an ideal or a doctrine, but in the give-and-take of human relations. He may say with sober relativism, "We need not hope in order to act, nor need we succeed in order to persevere,"[4] but he is seeking nevertheless the substance of a reality which will claim his allegiance, and to which the future belongs, in the business of daily human life.

CHRISTIANS IN THE SECULUM

We have described secularization as a movement away from religious world views in theory and away from the dominance of religious institutions in practice. This means, in large parts of the world, a movement away from Christianity and the authority of the church. Those historians have been largely right who have described it as a drama of Christendom, imported in an advanced state of development into cultures which had never known the dichotomy of religious and secular before.

But now we must say more than this. Theologically perceived, the proclamation of the Christian gospel is responsible for the dynamic of secularization, and is its first agent. This is so, even when those who carry it have no idea of producing these consequences, because the process begins with the history of the Hebrew people— with the calling of Moses and the revelation at Sinai— and is fulfilled in the incarnation of Jesus Christ and is expressed by the sanctifying work of the Holy Spirit in the church. To put it bluntly, the secularized state of human mind and society can be creative and is full of hope because it is the state into which God calls his people through their relation with him, and in which he sustains them by his grace. It is the attitude toward structures of thought and the common life which is most appropriate to the history and promise of that relationship. It is a quality of faith in believers and, where faith is not present, it is a condition in which, precisely for lack of any social and metaphysical obstructions, the word of God can be heard most clearly. Let us examine this thesis more closely.

Secularization begins with Biblical history. The Dutch philosopher Cornelis van Peursen suggests two forms of man's relation to objective reality which precede it: (a) the mythical, wherein man feels himself continuous with the nature and society around him, deriving his very sense of self from his participation in their forms; (b) the ontological, in which being is objective and accessible in its timeless substance to the human reason.[5] Arend van Leeuwen combines them both, on the basis of a comparative study of Hindu, Chinese, and early Mesopotamian civilization, into what he calls the "ontocratic pattern."[6] It is prebiblical, but it is also modern, a temptation and a tendency in primitive culture and modern social science.

From this base line the Biblical history departed, toward a totally new orientation to reality. The story of this is now familiar to Biblical scholars and cannot be told here in full.[7] We can only indicate its direction.

1. Man's efforts to lay hold of a structure of being which he himself would control, by grasping it with his mind (metaphysics) or by securing it with ceremonies and experiences (religion) were overturned by the way God revealed himself. One could illustrate almost at random from the Bible. When God first spoke to Abram there was no evidence of mystic illumination or of rational insight into eternal order; rather, the content of the address was command, "Go out from your kindred, from your father's house, to the land which I will show you," and promise, "And I will make of you a great nation . . . and in you shall all the families of the earth be blessed" (Gen. 12:1–2). The God who made himself known to Moses introduced himself historically: "I am the God of your father," and specifically refused to answer the question about his name, except in historical terms (Ex. 3:14–17).

2. As with the being of God, so also with nature and history, reflected in the human activities of economics and science, politics and culture. The Biblical basis of human knowledge and action in all these spheres is the relation which God establishes with his people, known as covenant. The Biblical covenant is first a personal relation. The reality it reflects is that of the personal claim of another on us as free and responsible agents. But it is also a relation between God and a community of believers through which his relation to the whole human world is expressed; and it is a dynamic, active relation which expresses itself in events to which structures of society and the stuff of the material world are instrumental.

Once again, the Biblical history is the story of human attempts to capture this relationship in sacred structures of political or natural order, and of God's judgment on the structures which reestablish the community of faith in

a properly secularized world. We take three examples
which still play a role in our life today.

a. It is well known that the basic principles and prescriptions of human behavior known as the law play a
large part in Biblical, as in later Jewish and Christian,
history. The laws in the Old Testament, as the prescriptions for Christian behavior in the Pauline letters of the
New Testament, are of various kinds. They have borrowed heavily from the codes of surrounding peoples. In
some cases they represent improvements on those codes,
in others they reinforce the best available morality of
the time. In any event they were modified and even
reversed from time to time as historical conditions in
the covenant relation between God and his people
changed the response required. Ceremonial laws com-
manded at the time of the exodus became an offense to
the eighth-century prophets, as did commandments in
modified form for the postexilic Jews. The Ten Commandments were drastically modified by Jesus; in some cases,
as with the laws against killing, adultery, and covetous-
ness, they were given a new dimension; in others, as with
the Sabbath commandment and that on honoring parents,
they were sharply corrected. The moral law, in the Bible,
was basically those teachings (*torah*) which expressed
for a time and place, the quality of relation which God
had given with his covenant and which is made finally
clear in Jesus Christ.

In short, Biblical history secularizes the law. It also records revolts against this secularization. The book of
Deuteronomy records a legal reform whereby the people
of Judah hoped to make themselves acceptable to God,
only to be told by Jeremiah, "They have healed the hurt
of my people slightly saying 'peace, peace,' when there is
no peace" (Jer. 6:14). The law which Paul rejected was
of the same character. His "All things are lawful for me,
but not all things are expedient" (I Cor. 6:12) expresses

exactly the congruence of Biblical and modern secular attitudes. Law is, and should be, the servant of expediency.

b. The Biblical story also secularizes nature. It places creation—the physical world—in the context of the covenant relation and does not try to understand it apart from that relation. The history of God with his people has a setting, and this setting is created nature. But the movement of history, not the structure of the setting, is central to reality. Physical creation even participates in this history; its timeless or cyclical character, so far as it exists, is unimportant. The physical world, in other words, does not have its meaning in itself. There are no spirits at work in it which can help or harm mankind. It is the creation of God alone and is the object of his manipulation.

c. The Biblical history secularizes the forms of the community of believers itself. This has been the hardest lesson of all for believers to learn. The people of Israel did not believe the prophets who prophesied the victory of their enemies because God, in their minds, was bound to his temple and to the prosperity and security of the people he had chosen. Even the disciples throughout the life of Jesus were thinking in terms of the Kingdom of God as a sacred order which he would bring in: "Grant us to sit, one at your right hand and one at your left, in your glory" (Mark 10: 37). And Paul was at constant odds with the sacralists to whom he himself brought the gospel: "Already you are filled! Already you have become . . . kings! And would that you did reign, so that we might share the rule with you!" (I Cor. 4: 8). Over against all this the covenant shows itself to be an ever-changing relation, the constancy of which lies in the character of God and not in the structure of the community.

The church is the community which cannot escape knowing all this, and which is called first to apply it to its own life. It lives by its participation in the death and resurrection of Christ in the Lord's Supper (Holy Communion, Eucharist). Its worship is a hearing and a responding to the word of God preached in its midst. These two acts give to the church itself a functional, secular existence. Because of them the church lives by rediscovering itself as judged and renewed by the work of Christ, by the transformation—potentially the transformation of the world—which goes on in its midst.

SECULAR THEOLOGY

This sets the terms of the theological task in modern society. We close with some suggestions on its content and direction.

1. We are left by the whole history we have described with the question of the reality of God. We say "reality" rather than "being," "essence," or "nature" in a deliberate effort to avoid the kind of thinking we have hitherto called metaphysical. We mean by it that long tradition of deductive system-building based on the first principles of thought and being, which is associated with the names of Aristotle and Plato, with the Greek church fathers and with Thomas Aquinas, with Descartes, Spinoza, and Leibniz, and subjected to basic criticism by Kant. The secular mind and Biblical revelation are at one in rejecting the way of thinking which this system-building requires, and the understanding of reality which is associated with it. Neither God nor his creation reveal to the human mind the structure of their essential being, for the very idea of such a structure or essence is a product of the human mind and therefore the instrument of man's desire to make his own ways sacred or absolute. The metaphysical task in the secular context then must be differently conceived—as the task of clarifying and relating ideas about man's situation within the limits of a particular position and bias in human history. Its point of reference will not be an ultimate structure of being but the

dynamic relations of this history and the responses it brings forth.[8]

We know the reality of God only in and through his acts in history, his covenant relation with man, his calling, judging, forgiving, reconciling, and saving acts toward society, centrally expressed in the life, death, resurrection, and coming again of Jesus Christ. Through these acts and in this relation we know him to be free sovereign Lord over creation, man, and history. The words we use to describe him—just, merciful, loving, and the like—are not definitions, but themselves expressions of our relation, and pointers to a reality which transcends our comprehension. Nevertheless, we know God as truly and wholly present with us, not partially removed into a mystical absolute. "God is who he is in the deed of his revelation," writes Karl Barth.[9]

This reality is differently perceived from most objects of human knowledge. He who acknowledges it lives within it. It lays claim on his actions; he understands himself and his world as part of this history. It is not a doctrine the truth of which he demonstrates, but a relation which he explores with his mind and expresses with his responsible life. For him "the will of God is what God does in all that nature and men do. It is the universal that contains, transforms, includes and fashions every particular."[10] He does not comprehend it or control it from God's perspective. He reckons with and depends on it as God's gift.

This is conventionally known as the response of faith. It is not, however, optional for secular man. In his specialized fields of activity, in the variety of his human relations, in the use of the power in his hands and in his free responsibility, the question cannot be avoided: What is the character of the reality with which I will reckon here? It is first a practical question. It is answered in the way money is spent—in families or in the budgets of nations. It is answered in the way machines are built and handled, and in the direction of research. It is answered in the way of a man with a woman, in lifelong marriage or passing relation. It may well be that most of us at this level are practical polytheists. Our realities clash and jostle, and we acknowledge them all. But it is the most responsible secular man whom this satisfies least, for he is left with the question of the integrity of his human responsibility itself. There is a law in me or in my mind, the law of my integrity; and there are many laws in my members, the laws of response to many systems of action about me. In my responsiveness and responsibility to the many I am irresponsible to the One beyond the many; I am irresponsible as a self, however responsible the natural, the political, the domestic, the biological complexes in me may be in relation to the systems of nature, or to the closed societies of nation, church, family, or profession, or to the closed society of life itself.[11]

The problem of reality in secular terms is the problem of the one Other to whom I as a whole human being am responsible, in and through the actions I perform and the other responsibilities I bear.

2. We are left with the question, then, of the secular reality of man. Toward this the whole foregoing discussion points. "The being of man is the history," writes Karl Barth, "in which one of God's creatures is elected and called by God, is included in his self-responsibility before God, and in which he shows himself qualified for this call and task."[12] The reference is of course to Jesus Christ. It would be incomprehensible were we to think of God, Christ, or man as substances with attributes. In fact, however, it expresses the heart of the dynamic relation of all three. Christ, says Bonhoeffer, is "the man-for-other-men." This is his character. It describes the innermost quality which his acts and relations revealed. As such he revealed also the decision of God to be for man, epitomized the meaning of all the full-bodied terms—holiness, righteousness, mercy, loving-kindness—with which the Old Testa-

ment had tried to express this relation. Man then is defined—given his existence, calling, and destiny—by his relation to the action of this God in Christ. In this action the whole world is included in its secularity and man is turned toward it as servant and witness by virtue of being "in Christ."

Man exists, then, as Christian faith sees it, in a field of personal relationships at the center of which is Jesus Christ. He is constituted in his very being by his actions and responses in that field. From him we derive our power to be human and our ever-changing understanding, in specific relations, of what it means. Through his work God negates the power of our inhumanity, releases us from fear of ourselves, and frees us to shoulder responsibility and take action which serves our neighbor, even when we incur guilt thereby. Because Christ is there, man is not an individual, nor part of the masses, nor the creature of a race or culture, nor the citizen of a nation, but a person in these various contexts, free for the responsibilities they carry because he is free from defining himself in terms of them.

3. The question of an authentically secular society receives thereby a theological answer. Society—the political and economic structures of the common life and the cultural habits and values which give it a sense of unity—is a creative task given to man, not a structure to be received. It is a Christian responsibility to help the secular world to remain truly secular when it itself is tempted to lose confidence in itself and to give way to new ideologies or myths.

The church participates with every secular society in its search for justice and freedom for all its people. As this involves social analysis, political action, and formulation of the particular hope of that people, it may mean many an ideological risk. But the church and its theology have the task of reminding such a society that its focus is the true need of man, that its function is the cultivation and development of personal relations among its members in free and experimental interaction. They have the task of warning the commonwealth whenever human beings are in danger of being sacrificed to institutions, projects, or ideas. They have the task of confronting such a society through the church's own life and thought with the vision of what man is, the purpose for which he lives, in Jesus Christ, and with the continual self-criticism and reform which this involves. The final point will attempt to spell out one illustration of what this implies.

4. In no area of society are the problems of responsible action more baffling or the situation more dangerous than in the sphere of national and international politics. This is partly because power which can destroy the world is located here, but also because it has been so incompletely secularized. Many political ideologies have lost their convincing power; indeed, we owe the precarious peace of coexistence to the fact that this is so. But mythology, especially of the secular religion of nationalism, persists even among those who no longer believe it, and political decisions are made which reflect illusions more than reality. The present writer is an American. What he says will inevitably reflect that country's experience. But it may still be of some more general value to pose the question from one setting: What is a Christian's responsibility for his country's policy?

First, he is called to act as a solvent of the nation's remaining ideological illusions. When several years ago George F. Kennan propounded the thesis that foreign policy must be based frankly on a nation's self-interest, and not on moral principle, he was speaking as a responsible Christian. When a nation sets up its own national morality—even its concepts of freedom, justice, and peace —as a universal standard by which to measure others, this self-justification becomes the heart of disobedience to God. In fact, a nation is, like its citizens, a self-interested body, whose insight into the truth about world order and whose morals in working for it are highly relative. It lives in a world of other such nations with which it must interact. The Christian is called to prepare the nation to see the judgment and calling of God in the give-and-take of world affairs, in the defeats as well as the victories of its policies. As a secular institution the nation is not absolute. Loyalty to it must be critical and qualified, in order that it may better serve its proper limited purposes, as one expression of responsible community among men.

Second, the Christian is deeply involved in the responsibility which his nation has for using what power is at its command to serve human need. From this responsibility there is no withdrawal without unfaithfulness to God and to one's fellowman. Having said this, however, let us be clear that there is a radical difference between a nation's self-interested use of power and the use of it which God intends. The power of foreign aid is a major example. Christians are in the position therefore of continually seeking to help the nation to reinterpret its self-interest in terms more inclusive of the needs and interests of others, and at the same time holding up the mirror of Christ to all self-interest as a judgment and a stimulus to the imagination. The nation will always argue that its most creative and altruistic policies are consistent with its self-interest. The church lives from the conquest of its self-interest by the power of Christ, on which the peace of the world depends. By the continual operation of this tension the policies of the nation are made fruitful.

Third, the Christian, fully involved with his nation's capacity to make war—in this case possibly nuclear war— bears witness to the nation of the relativity of all conflict to the purpose of reconciliation. No nation is righteous enough to seek an unconditional surrender. No cause is just enough to excuse any means of conflict to fight it. Because Christ has brought peace to all men there are no absolute conflicts or enmities. There are also no absolute governments. It may be that a nation must fight at times for people—its own or others. But then the welfare of the people must be the test of the battle and of the terms on which it ends.

Finally, the Christian recognizes that political power, like all power, has its limits. It can coerce, but rarely heal. It can set limits to human behavior, but rarely win people's allegiance. It can put down rebellions, but it cannot —at least American power cannot—produce a social revolution. Secular reality in politics includes the moment when the most creative political action is to renounce power and to bear witness in defenseless service to the human relations one seeks to establish. There are times— and there are nations which have lived through them —when the only wise political act is to suffer injustice and oppression not in hate but in forgiveness and inner freedom, out of which a new relationship may grow. Here also the pattern of secular reality is the pattern of the man-for-other-men. Secular men in any situation can see the human logic of this. But that this pattern contains hope, that the future belongs to the reality we find in this man, is a truth for which there is no proof; there is only witness. This is perhaps the irreducible Christian contribution to the integrity of the secular community—to live within it ourselves, in all its incoherent functionality, in all its appalling responsibility for power and for powerlessness, in all its search for particular forms of humanness, as men who see by faith a promise here which is based on analyses of social trends, but which comes to all of us from without. If we live by the reality of this future we shall be secular men but we shall not be conformed to "the world," for we shall be looking at it from the angle of its meaning and direction given by that acting reality whom we call God. By the never-ceasing operation of this tension in all who believe, the secular life of the world is made fruitful.

Religion, Morality,
and Secularization

THOUGH IT IS notoriously difficult to find a precise or
generally acceptable definition of "secularization," we are
not totally at sea. There are certain aspects of our social
experience that such a term rather obviously describes.
Without trying to be at all exhaustive, we shall identify
some of these aspects and then draw a few conclusions.

Common sense seems to tell us that, at least as con-
trasted with earlier periods in our history, one area of
social life in which religious appeals, or appeals to an
independent sacred realm, play a decreasingly important
role is moral belief and practice. Even hasty reflection on
Western history, right up to the modern period, indicates
that religious control over moral life is not what it used
to be. Time was when a man could be punished by law
for blasphemy or spotty church attendance. Moreover,
the reasons given for legal as well as moral prescriptions
against murder, lying, adultery, failure to observe the
Sabbath, and so on, were likely to be religious reasons
as well as secular, or utilitarian, ones. In the Puritan colonies, for example, and well up into nineteenth-century
America, the fact that the "God of our fathers" had laid
down his Ten Commandments, and had promised to enforce them if the political authorities did not, was one
important reason for subscribing to the moral law.

Nowadays in our pluralistic society, to try to justify
moral and legal prescriptions that apply to all Americans
—like those in favor of fair treatment or equal opportuni-

Previously unpublished.

ties or religious liberty—by invoking a particular religious tradition has an air of quaintness about it. Of what particular relevance to the moral life or the legal obligations of the agnostic or the Jew is an appeal to the love or the wrath of the God of Jesus Christ? Such an appeal is about as useful as the words of the United States senator who urged the Israelis and the Arabs to settle their differences "according to Christian principles." While religious warrants are no doubt still persuasive *within* particular religious communions and thus of consequence in motivating religious people to act morally, they have ever weaker force outside the given communions. Accordingly, Americans have gradually been compelled to search for grounds of moral belief and practice outside their individual religious traditions. Whatever else it may have been, the secularization of morality has been a practical necessity in modern American life.

We may, therefore, propose our own (limited) definition of "secularization" as follows: *It is the process by which coercive religious controls over the moral beliefs and practices of a given society are reduced.* Since the word "coercive" will function prominently in our analysis, it requires special comment. I mean by "coercion" the capacity of a given agent, whether an individual, divine or human, or an institution, such as a church or state, to impose its will by resorting to the threat or use of physical punishment. A "sacred" society, as opposed to a "secular" one, is a society in which religious definitions of moral belief and practice are capable of being coercively enforced, if need be.

I want further to stress what seems to me to be the close connection, certainly in the Judeo-Christian tradition, between divine and worldly-political coercion. It is no accident that precisely in those historical periods when God's wrath and his last judgment and punishment are emphasized, there is a concomitant urgency for political-legal enforcement of his commands. It is not hard to understand why this is so. Considering what God's punishment is likely to be, political authorities have a responsibility to use all the means in their power to prevent men from pursuing practices that can bring them nothing but the eternal terror of an angry God. Thus does a political-legal image of God, as is found in parts of the Old Testament, in the world view of the Middle Ages, and in aspects of Puritanism, reinforce a view of morality that is governed by the close cooperation of the religious and political authorities. Incidentally, a close association between religion and politics is not peculiar to Judaism and Christianity, but can be found in different forms in classical Hinduism, and in aspects of Buddhism, Confucianism, and Islam. As Max Weber pointed out in his essays on the sociology of religion, for all these religions moral prescriptions are justified at least partly on religious grounds and enforced, to a greater or lesser extent, by the political-legal agencies.[1]

One thing that appears clear about the contemporary drift of American religion is the tendency to de-emphasize a coercive and punitive God at the same time as religious definitions of morality are decreasingly enforced by the state. That is, physical punishment or deprivation becomes a much less frequent reason for behaving morally, whether punishment is defined in this-worldly or otherworldly terms. Certainly hell and damnation are not often invoked these days to encourage religious people to perform their moral duties, at least not in main-line Protestant pulpits. As we have said, it was not always so.

Now some people argue that as the coercive sanctions of religious morality decline, as they assuredly have in modern society, we are at the same time witnessing the end of any connection between religion and morality. In this sense, the secularization of morality is alleged to mean the complete decline of the moral significance of religion. After all, runs this line of argument, religion pictures to the believer an external or "heteronomous" or "paternalistic" authority over against him that commands certain actions and attitudes after the fashion of a father commanding his son. Behind these commands there is all the while the threat of severe sanctions for disobedience. As the result of just such reasoning, P. H. Nowell-Smith, the British philosopher, has contended that *all* religious morality "is infantile."[2] Religion does not foster "independent" or "autonomous" or "free" moral agents who act because they see the point of their action and do it for that reason. Rather, they act from fear or from a sense of dependency on the law of another, which is, of course, what "hetero-nomos" means.

> The idea of heteronomy is . . . strongly marked in Christian morality. "Not as I will, but as thou wilt." . . . It is the total surrender of the *will* that is required. . . . If we dare to ask why, the only answer is "Have faith"; and faith is an essentially heteronomous idea; for it is not a reasoned trust in someone in whom we have good grounds for reposing trust; it is blind faith, utter submission of our own reason and will.[3]

This sort of morality is still grounded in the coercive power of the "other" to enforce his commands. Consequently, for Nowell-Smith, the decline of religion means the decline of heteronomy and the coming of age of modern man. There are obvious parallels here with the thought of the "secular Christians" in the tradition of Dietrich Bonhoeffer.

It is worth noting that on the sociological side, Glock and Stark predict that a radical alteration of the traditional supernatural beliefs of Christianity will be necessary to accommodate the new emphasis upon what they call ethicalism within the churches, or a growing concern with social justice and the creation of a humane society.[4]

> The ethically oriented Christian seems to be deterred rather than challenged by what he finds in church. The more a man is committed to ethicalism, the less likely he is to contribute funds or participate in the life of the church.

We suspect that, in the long run, he is also less likely to remain a member. . . . Individual church members whose religious beliefs are the least orthodox score higher on ethicalism than the most orthodox.[5]

There seems a profound tension in contemporary American churches between the moral innovators and activists on the one side and those members who still manifest a strong allegiance to traditional religious beliefs on the other. Presumably, the former group will be much less likely than the latter to give clearly religious reasons for its behavior.

However, despite the arguments of Nowell-Smith, as well as those of Glock and Stark, it does not appear to me that there is any *necessary* reason why religion, and particularly the Christian tradition, must lose all moral significance under the undeniable pressure of secularization. On the contrary, I shall contend that at least the Christian tradition has had, and continues to have, a positive stake in the maintenance and extension of "secularization" in the sense we have defined it.

To begin with, I believe Talcott Parsons is right when he contends that the primitive Christian church made a very revolutionary contribution to the development of Western moral understanding and practice by institutionalizing a "new autonomy" in social relationships.[6] Parsons argues that this revolution was accomplished, in part, by creating a distinctive community that was self-consciously *differentiated* from the institutions of political-legal coercion. The well-known Biblical injunction, "Render to Caesar the things that are Caesar's, and to God the things that are God's," lays the foundations for distinguishing between behavior justified on specifically religious grounds that are selected and affirmed on the basis of personal choice and behavior that is enforced by the physical sanctions of the state.

It was the emergence of the primitive ecclesia—or the community of those "called out"—that posed a profound threat to the moral patterns of both Rome and Judaism in the first century. Each society was in its way what we designated as a sacred society, or one in which religious definitions of moral belief and practice are subject to coercive enforcement. In Rome, especially under the deified authority of Caesar Augustus, "the empire was, in effect, a politico-ecclesiastical institution. It was a Church as well as a State."[7] An inscription from 2 B.C. reinforces this point:

> The eternal and deathless nature of the universe has perfected its immense benefits to mankind in granting us a supreme benefit, for our happiness and welfare, Caesar Augustus, Father of his own Fatherland, divine Rome, Zeus Paternal, and Savior of the whole human race, in whom Providence has not only fulfilled but even surpassed the prayers of all men.[8]

While it is true that Imperial Rome made room for private clubs and mystery religions that were to some degree independent of the state, these communities were radically different from the early Christian communities in that they did not prevent their "adherents from joining in the official cultus of the city state. . . ."[9] For all but the Christian church (and the Jewish congregations, for different reasons), both religious and political loyalty could be centered in the state cult without any difficulty. It was undoubtedly because of their resistance at this point that the early Christians, much more than other groups, encountered such intense hostility at the hands of the Roman state.

Though in its own form and practices very different from "eternal Rome," first-century Judaism was a sacred society through and through. As Joseph Klausner describes it, "Judaism [was] not only religion and only ethics; it [was] the sum total of all the needs of a nation, placed on a religious basis."[10] The intense Maccabean impulse in postexilic Judaism made this point dramatically clear: here was a national or political religion par excellence. To observe the practical and ritualistic details of the Jewish law was both a religious and a political-legal obligation. A first-century Jew would not have understood how religious and political behavior could have been separated.

So long as religious and moral beliefs and practices are directly related to and enforced by political-legal authority, the opportunity for personal (or "autonomous") choice is severely restricted. By undermining this direct relation, the Christian church significantly broadened the range of opportunity for personal choice and, in fact, put a new premium on personal responsibility in religious and moral affairs. It would be hard to read the Gospels or Paul's Letters without observing the unrelieved emphasis upon the requirement of personal repentence and commitment. Unlike the political religions of Roman or Jewish society, the Christian religion demanded that one make an individual decision to adopt the Christian life, a decision that was often contrary to the inclinations of the state.

The effect of this development was, as C. N. Cochrane has pointed out, the secularization of the political order.[11] Under the pressure of the Christian movement, the jurisdiction of the state was restricted; the political-legal institutions were robbed of their full sacral authority. Tertullian's famous words underscore the point:

> I am willing to call the Emperor Lord but only in the conventional sense, never in the sense in which I accord that title to the Omnipotent and Eternal who is his Lord as well as mine. . . . Accordingly we follow the apostolic injunction to submit to magistracies . . . *but only within the limits of discipline;* that is, so long as we keep ourselves clear of idolatry.[12]

Political obligation was now limited by a higher obligation, one that was identified in the ecclesia.

Logically, at least, this worked the other way as well. If the political-legal authorities might no longer have full responsibility for religious and moral matters, neither might they be required to enforce specifically Christian definitions of religion and morals. Though Christians would have a very hard time learning the lesson, the clear implication of primitive Christianity is that a voluntary church promotes a voluntary religion. Not only must one have the option to choose the faith. The only proper way the faith may be appropriated and maintained is by *personal consent*. The possibility of dissent as well as consent must therefore always exist, and there is no such possibility where Christianity or any other faith is a state religion. It is true that historically Christians have gravitated again and again toward collapsing this crucial distinction between church and state. But, as Troeltsch saw so perceptively, this inclination seems always to provoke a countervailing tendency in Christendom in favor of the voluntary religion we are stressing. We shall comment later on one example of this phenomenon in the tensions between English Puritanism and Anglicanism.

However, with all the importance placed on personal responsibility for religious and moral choices, early Christianity was anything but a religion of solitary individuals. Paul's Letters make unmistakable that the Christian gains his new autonomy in an autonomous community. By differentiating itself, though not entirely divorcing itself, from the political community, the church cultivated the consciousness and the practice of "consensual self-government." In the first place, membership in the community was to be determined solely by personal consent, and not by inherited ethnic or political identity. There was, to be sure, some resistance on this point, but it was decisively overcome in the confrontation between Peter and Paul at Antioch (Gal., ch. 2; cf. ch. 3:23–29).

In the second place, the primitive church institutionalized what Bultmann has called "congregational democracy."[13] It was by no means present unambiguously, but it was there, particularly in Paul, and it rested on the assumption that roles and statuses within the community "are all . . . fundamentally equal, and superiority and subordination are to be regarded as only incidental."[14] The aristocratic and monarchic tendencies of ecclesiastical administration were never able to eliminate entirely these patterns of consensual participation that have manifested themselves again and again in certain monastic movements, in conciliarism, in Anabaptism, and in aspects of Calvinism and Puritanism.

It seems clear, in short, that the primitive Christian movement was a positive secularizing agent in that it helped to differentiate, in sociological terms, between political-legal coercion and religious and moral life, and thereby it increased the chances for a new autonomy in religion and morals.

However, with this more or less sociological description of primitive Christianity, we have not yet touched the heart of the point made by Nowell-Smith, that when all is said and done all religious morality—including Christianity—is heteronomous and infantile. To our argument so far he might simply respond that the alleged new autonomy created by Christianity is in reality a new heteronomy. That is, he might admit that primitive Christianity did contribute to the secularization of the Roman Empire by setting up a new authority over against the authority of the emperor. But, he might suggest, that is but to replace one authoritarian figure with another. The God of Jesus Christ took the place of Augustus or the Jewish law and nation as the source of moral authority. If Christianity pressed toward a greater range of personal independence in religion and morals than, say, first-century Judaism, it was still a moral position that was grounded in abject dependence on an authoritarian God.

If this is a correct application of Nowell-Smith's view, I believe the view is seriously one-sided, and therefore

badly oversimplifies the Christian point of view. I want
to try to show that the new autonomy engendered by the
primitive Christian movement was not simply the product
of certain accidental sociological occurrences but was also
the product of a particular way of reasoning about religion and morals. This way of reasoning, I believe, worked
against whatever authoritarian or heteronomous tendencies existed in early Christian thinking.

First of all, it does seem clear that there are several
patterns of religious and moral reasoning in the New
Testament. One pattern appears close to the "paternalistic" brand of religious morals Nowell-Smith has in mind.
That is, the picture of a divine "Father" or "Judge" who
dispenses rewards for good behavior and threatens dire
punishment for bad is not altogether foreign to the Synoptics or to Paul.[15] To the extent that the motif of rewards
and punishments is employed in the New Testament to
motivate believers to obey the commands of God, I agree
that we continue to have a heteronomous ethic in the
New Testament. To that extent, coercive religious controls
do still prevail over moral beliefs and practices, except
that the coercive controls are defined supernaturally. They
will be administered "in the Last Day" instead of here
and now, by the human authorities.

But to limit the religious and moral reasoning of the
New Testament to this one pattern is a distortion. Of
much greater prominence, at least in the thought of Paul,
and to a lesser degree in the Synoptics, is a pattern we
may entitle "the morality of gratitude." This pattern is of
quite a different order from the image Nowell-Smith has
of Christian morality. It makes very little room for rewards and punishments as the foundation of morality.

For Paul, the Christian has an obligation, perhaps more
than anything else, to be grateful to God for what he has
already done on behalf of man. The whole point of the
first chapter of Romans, for example, is to establish the
justice of God's cause against man in terms of man's in-

gratitude. God makes the first move by creating the world and giving man his life. And although all men had every reason to appreciate the gift as well as the giver, "they did not honor him . . . or give thanks to him" (Rom. 1:21). "Since they did not see fit to acknowledge God, God gave them up to a base mind and to improper conduct" (Rom. 1:28). In other words, human disobedience is the result of this underlying ingratitude, and until that is rectified disobedience and unlawful conduct will not be overcome.

By all rights, men deserve severe punishment for their ingratitude, but God makes yet a second benevolent move on man's behalf: he "gives up" his Son "by his grace as a gift" (Rom. 3:24). What is now required as well as made possible in Christ is the proper spirit of gratitude that was due from the beginning. On the model of Christ's life and death, man's appropriate response can now be "freely given" or given with heartfelt consent (II Cor. 3:1–6). A grudging response, or a response that is dictated by the fear of punishment, is precisely what is *not* appropriate. The very "curse" of the law, as Paul understands it, is that it has become a heteronomous or coercive force regulating man's moral life according to the threat of eternal wrath.

This whole way of arguing is neatly summarized in Paul's words to the Corinthians: "What have you that you did not receive? If then you received it, why do you boast as if it were not a gift?" (I Cor. 4:7). The point is that the appeal is manifestly not to the threat of punishment or other coercive controls, divine or human, but simply to the logic of gratitude itself. If we were to reconstruct it, the argument would proceed something like this: It is assumed that men have an obligation to respond to benevolent acts in a spirit of gratitude; God has acted with great benevolence on man's behalf; therefore man is obligated to respond gratefully to God.

Though it is perhaps incomplete,[16] this is a very suggestive moral argument, especially in the light of the themes we are emphasizing. As Paul intuits, the obligation of gratitude is an unusual and very delicate sort of obligation. On the one hand, we, like Paul, feel justified in calling people to account—for example, children—if they do not "give thanks" or "acknowledge" a benefactor. To label someone an ingrate is not a mild form of rebuke. On the other hand, there is something self-defeating about trying to coerce a person to be grateful by means of punishment or condemnation. "You ought to *want* to thank him for his kindness; I should not have to tell you to do it," we often say to children. In short, gratitude—if it is to be genuine—must be *self-initiated,* must come from the heart, must be freely given. If it is coerced or grudging, it is not gratitude at all. As we saw, Paul was wrestling with this tension in the logic of gratitude between requiring thankfulness and encouraging it as a free response.

Beyond this, Kant makes a comment about gratitude that is directly relevant to Paul's whole orientation. "One cannot," says Kant, "by any requital of a kindness received, rid oneself of the obligation for this kindness, since one can never win away from the benefactor his *priority* of merit: the merit of having been the first in benevolence."[17] One is always eager to repay a benefactor, but never can, precisely because the benefactor *made the first move.* This fact about gratitude helps to explain the asymmetrical relationship between God and man in Paul's view: God made the prior move on man's behalf, and nothing man might do could ever overcome God's priority of merit. The best man can do is to remain eternally grateful.

Though this excursion into the morality of gratitude must remain sketchy, we have introduced it so as to expose the inadequacies of Nowell-Smith's view of Christian morality. It ought to be plain now that insofar as this emphasis was operative, Paul's understanding of religion and morals was by no means exclusively heteronomous. It is not necessarily based on unreasoned trust or blind faith in an authoritarian figure whose authority to command rests in his power to coerce and to punish. On the contrary, as we have argued, God's authority is established, above all, by his priority of merit, by his own self-initiated (or uncoerced) benevolence on behalf of man. Against this background, man has, according to Paul, a perfectly good reason for responding with heartfelt gratitude, namely because of the benefits that God has already bestowed upon man. This is the same good reason that most of us would give for recommending gratitude in the face of any genuinely gracious or gift-giving act.

Though I have no space to develop the idea, it is my conviction that Paul extends the logic of gratitude to include not only obligations between God and man, but also between man and man. The whole discussion of proper social relationships in Rom., ch. 12, and I Cor., ch. 12, is couched in the language of gift-giving and receiving. "There are varieties of gifts, but the same Spirit; and there are varieties of service, but the same Lord" (I Cor. 12:4). That is, in Paul's way of thinking, in the ideal community men will regard others as "a gift," and, accordingly, the various aspects of the obligation of gratitude that we have been exploring will become the appropriate form of social response.

The main point of all this is that to shape religious and moral understanding according to the logic of gratitude, as Paul does, is to remove, now at the theoretical level, the grounds for coercive religious controls over moral belief and practices, and to develop the foundation for a new autonomy in religion and morals. In the first place, it is clear that the virtue of gratitude, as we have analyzed it, is in no sense "infantile." In fact, it is no accident that expressions of genuine gratitude come so hard to small children. That children so frequently must be prompted or shamed by another into saying thank you for gracious acts, rather than doing so of their own accord, suggests that gratitude presupposes a rather high level of moral maturity.

Moreover, to emphasize the logic of gratitude is to make room for and, indeed, to intensify personal or self-initiated moral responsibility. Because genuine gratitude cannot, by definition, be externally coerced, the conditions are created that put a premium on the opportunity for free or autonomous responses. And, as we saw above, the opportunity for freedom and consent entails the possibility of dissent, or the possibility to make other than predetermined choices.

I am arguing, then, that to the extent that secularization means the reduction of coercive religious controls over morals, there are significant themes within primitive Christianity that contribute positively to the secularization process. This is true, we have contended, both at the sociological or institutional level and at the theoretical level. By no means do I wish to overreact to Nowell-Smith's distortions with an equally one-sided account of my own. I have admitted the partial truth of some of his arguments. But there is much more to primitive Christianity than Nowell-Smith understands. It seems clear that those crucial aspects of Western secularized morality—voluntary (or uncoerced) religion and freedom of conscience—are but the logical extension of some central themes in the New Testament. It is in part for these reasons that I dissent from the notion that the secularization of morality *necessarily* means the decline or the rejection of the moral significance of Christianity.

Max Weber rightly saw that English Puritanism, by elaborating and institutionalizing certain important features of the Christian tradition, contributed uniquely to the secularization process in seventeenth-century England and America. However, he devoted his attention to the connections between Puritanism and the rise of rational capitalism. He did not focus particularly on the relationship of Puritanism to the rise of secularized morality. Had he done so, he would, I believe, have discovered that the Puritans were, in their own circumstances, recapturing and freshly applying some of the themes we have discovered in primitive Christianity, and thereby making their own contribution to the removal of coercive religious controls over moral life. Though the story is much more complex than I can go into here, let me briefly suggest how this was so, both at the institutional and at the theoretical levels.

So far as the institutions were concerned, Anglican England, against which Puritanism mounted its crusade, was a "sacred society" in every sense of the word.[18] Politics and religion were inextricably intertwined, for in the Elizabethan Settlement the crown was adjudged to be supreme in things ecclesiastical as well as temporal. Puritanism in all its forms was concerned to separate or differentiate the relationship between church and state, though some Puritans wished to go much farther than others in this regard. Over and over, the Puritans stressed the centrality of a voluntary and consensual faith instituted in a voluntary and consensual church. In order to achieve this pattern, political-legal coercion would have to be put in its place. That is, it was not the office of the state to make final determinations regarding matters of faith and morals. That was the province of relatively autonomous church bodies.

Though all Puritans shared these views, some were more radical than others in seeking to implement them. The so-called left-wing Puritans took the full consequences of this outlook. Groups like "the Levellers" urged a radical separation of church and state, complete religious toleration ("All sects were to be free, and Catholics, Jews and Turks as well"), and free, consensually determined religious groups. As they put it in 1649:

We do not empower and entrust our government to make any laws or covenants whereby to compel, by penalties or otherwise, any person from the profession of his faith or the exercise of his religion according to his conscience, nothing having caused more destructions and heart burnings in all ages than molestation for matters of conscience in and about religion.

Moreover, the radical Puritans attempted to extend the patterns of consensualism in church affairs to the organization of the secular government. It seems clear that this stress on voluntary religion and free conscience helped to encourage the sort of secularized morality that was shortly to be articulated by John Locke in works such as his *Letter Concerning Toleration.*

Though it is true that theologically the Puritans placed great emphasis upon a heteronomous God, whose threats of punishments added an unmistakably coercive dimension to Puritan morality, my inkling is that, as is true in the case of the New Testament, the place of supernatural punishment and psychological dread in Puritanism has been overstressed.[19] For lack of sufficient investigation, my judgment here must remain tentative, but it seems likely that quotations such as the following one from William Perkins, an eminent Puritan divine, are not unusual:

Because we are freed from the bondage of the law, therefore we must be a law to ourselves; we must be voluntaries, without constraint, freely yielding subjection to the will of God *and not for fear of hell, and the last judgment.*[20]

We could hardly find a clearer expression of the new autonomy that seems to be a central feature both of secularized morality and of the Christian faith.

VIII

Julian N. Hartt

Secularity and the Transcendence of God

I

THE AIM of this essay is to render a constructive account of Christian belief in God Transcendent. The use of the word "theological" is intended to distinguish this venture both from sociological inquiry and from philosophical speculation. I do not understand the distinction to be absolute, however. The Christian and the church need a firm foundation on which to construe the cultural situation; and today this means some kind of response to secularity. Hence the treatment accorded here to secularity is likely to bear some resemblance to sociological generalization. Moreover, Christian belief in God Transcendent is a case of metaphysical belief; and so the speculative philosopher may keep a jealous eye on any invasion of his territory. But the cultural situation is not the property of sociology; and metaphysicians do not have a divine appointment to police beliefs about reality. Accordingly, so long as a theologian does not presume to instruct either sociologists or philosophers in their respective trades, he does not need to feel obliged to accept either as tutor in his own.

I propose therefore first to lay out some features of a Christian belief in God Transcendent. The second objective is to provide an account of secularity that concentrates on the religious features of this cultural situation.

Previously unpublished.

But this second objective is as theological as the first; for it is pursued with an eye on showing that the sense a Christian can discover in secularity is superior to the account a secularist provides of the same phenomenon.

II

Some sensationally easy victories over belief in God Transcendent have been scored by taking that belief at its picturesque worst. For example, Christians are represented as believing in a God who lives outside the world in a place called heaven from which he sends out mysterious messages, and into which place he will someday collect the souls of the people of whom he approves. It requires neither sociological nor theological genius to show that this picturesque nonsense can make no intelligible or productive contact with the spirit of secularity. But what is thus represented as the Christian view has an antecedent defect as well: it is a gross distortion of Christian belief in God Transcendent. That judgment must seem a flat and presumptuous assertion, presumptuous because it clearly hints that there is something Christians ought to believe whether or not they do. That there is such a rule of faith ought to be shown rather than merely asserted.

One way of showing it is to track down a meaning of transcendence that comports with the images of God in the New Testament, images that command and direct the attention of the Christian. This is the hazardous route I choose to follow here.

The principal image of God in the New Testament is a being of unchallengeable majesty and righteousness who binds himself to something he has created, thus securing the fulfillment of its essential possibility. It is therefore appropriate that this God should in good faith be called Father, Lord, Shepherd, since each such title in its own way calls attention to his self-binding pledge.

When thereafter it is said of God that he "dwells in light unapproachable" (I Tim. 6:16) and in him "there is no variation or shadow due to change" (James 1:17) the Christian ought not to take such cryptic utterances to be dogmatic definitions of divine transcendence. In that direction lie religious and philosophical notions incompatible with the principal image of God in the New Testament. But what are the other possibilities?

One: God transcends the world in that he rather than the world has what is needed for the fulfillment of the world.

This notion is sometimes expressed in a formula of doubtful value: The world needs (depends upon) God but God does not need the world. (World − God = 0. God − world = God.) This proposition suggests strongly that contemplation of a cosmic situation essentially different from the actual one would disclose an essential property of God's being, his aseity. So far as I can determine, the sole virtue of this speculation is that it might reinforce a religious intuition, i.e., that God is God no matter what happens in any actual or imaginable state of the universe. But it might also be construed as support for the notion that God could part with the world without the slightest sense of loss.

Two: God's goodness (or in more general terms, his value) surpasses the goodness of creation, in whole or in part; and this because there is no limit by which the goodness of God must be defined.

The heart of this notion is sometimes expressed thus: God has in himself all of the value realized in diffusion through the universe. But many zigs and zags are required to make the substitute formula plausible; and in the process the essential image may be lost. For shall we say that God has in himself the perfection of the blooming rose, in any sense other than his knowledge of that phenomenon and his good pleasure in it? It is truly unfortunate that divine transcendence should be conceived as requiring God to say to any creature, "Anything you can do I can do better!" We ought rather to represent God's good pleasure in the blooming rose as the best reason in the world for its being there.

Three: God transcends the world in that his wisdom in deploying his resources is unsurpassable, is indeed unapproachable, by any other being.

This notion is calculated to remind one that Christian belief in God Transcendent must resist powerful and subtle temptations to represent God as overwhelmingly powerful—able to do anything that occurs to him as being an opportunity to display his might—and thereafter as a being to be trusted and loved because of his unmatchable goodness. Perhaps there is comfort to be pressed out of the dialectical twin of this metaphysical-religious temptation: God in his righteousness is lovely beyond all mortal bearing, and just happens to have power sufficient for his impeccable purposes. The third option has thus something of a mediating function, largely because it is the very essence of wisdom to mediate rightness of principle and loftiness of purpose to the solid factuality of the world. A wise person is one who can correctly estimate what is the case and render efficaciously thereto his apprehension of and commitment to goodness. By definition God's knowledge of what is the case is faultless. Theologians concerned to maintain belief in God Transcendent must thereafter accept the task of showing how belief in his wisdom (that is, his unsurpassable mastery of the instruments appropriate for the realization of the loftiest ends) can be defended against the ever-mounting pressure of secularity.

This is what I shall now undertake. For the decisive New Testament image of God is that of a being of unapproachable righteousness and majesty of power who has thrown in his lot with the strangest of all his creations, man. And one of the oddest of all the achievements of secularity is a powerful, though hardly constant, conviction that such a gamble is anything but wise, whether made by men or gods.

III

What then is this cultural situation identified as secularity? The following components merit theological attention.

One: loss of confidence in traditional religious systems. We can safely leave to sociologists to determine whether people in this society are becoming less religious. In the meantime I think we can be sure that many no longer entrust to any traditional religious system any significant fraction of their economic, social, and political power. Again, this is not to say that the generality of people have lost their religious beliefs. In some intellectualistic circles, to have thrown off the dead weight of such beliefs is an indispensable criterion of spiritual maturity. This seems not to be true of society generally, though it may also be true of motorcycle gangs.

Two: widespread confidence in the powers of science to solve the most urgent problems, both cognitive and practical, now confronting Western man if not mankind generally. This component of secularity is the natural brother of the first one. The loss of confidence in traditional religious systems is not a clear philosophical victory over religious outlooks. Rather, it is a matter of one erstwhile powerful social system being replaced by another one; and these events are rarely if ever largely or clearly rational exchanges. Traditional religious systems have been found to be less and less effective in administering human power; and this, again, is because something else now seems clearly to be better for this purpose. The general public may be momentarily interested in a crashing triumph of research science if it is made minimally intelligible. "Science has solved the Riddle of Life!" "Science has created life in a test-tube!" "Science has discovered the cause of cancer!" Headlines such as these create sufficient interest in the general reader to induce him to read perhaps a third of the appropriate article, or at least look carefully at the revealing pictures and diagrams. But, "Astronauts land on the moon!" "Science can now let you choose the sex of your next baby!" "At last, a cure for cancer! (or for air pollution, sterility, impotency, poverty, etc.)"—*that* is the stuff of secularity, the cash-out of the scientific business in terms of prolongation of human life, the extension of the boundaries of human power, rendering man comfortable, safe, and free from servitude to demeaning tasks.

Thus, to the degree that traditional religious systems reinforced, if they did not exalt, the sense of human life as transitory, weak, and vulnerable, and sought therefore and thereby to keep it in bondage to a presumptively divine order—to that degree, at least, such systems have been discredited by the growth of science. The educated person now is amply armed against ancient definitions of man's limitations and of his nature and destiny overall. The person of properly educated sensibility may still believe part of that religious picture, but provisionally, for some scientific discovery may shortly knock out that residue too.

Accordingly, secularity denotes a very heavy dependence upon science for significant revisions of outlook and policy, rather than upon philosophy or religion; for neither philosophy nor religion has played an important or perhaps even a measurable role in the reshaping of the daily world. The scientist is the architect of this world. The contractor is the engineer. And the private creed of either or both is of no consequence as a factor in the prosecution of the social functions to which they are ordained.

Three: preoccupation with the daily world. We err when we construe this as a philosophic triumph of time over eternity, of nature over supernature, etc. Those heroic conflicts matter very little to the daily world. Whether it is made in an antic or in a solemn spirit, an announcement of the death of God may at the discretion of the editor be placed under either the religion or the obituary column. It would be read by more people if the latter, by the putatively more thoughtful if the former.

Four: preoccupation with effective instrumentalizing of unquestioned ends and taken-for-granted purposes. This is a prime feature of the daily world. In this we may begin to make out the dense and momentous connections of secularity with the daily world. I do not mean to suggest that long-standing views of man's proper end are still decisive in this age, for they are not. Rather, the point is, again, the role of science in the modern persuasion that the right order and volume of instruments is at last available for the perfection of human life. Indeed the point can legitimately be made stronger: the right attack on instrumentalization itself leads to the proper revision of ends and purposes. So again the inveterate disposition of religious systems to stress the fixity and finality of the human good as such runs afoul of a fundamental disposition of secularity.

It does not follow from this and it is probably not true that people generally (the denizens of the daily world) have become desensitized to religious experience as such. They may in fact crave more vividness and pungency in the line of religious experience than the traditional religious systems are providing.

Five: a quest for the holy beyond the precincts of the sacred. The traditional theological distinction, sacred/secular, does not throw much light on the daily world and the secular spirit. For that purpose much more needs to be made of the distinction holy/profane.

To hold something as holy is to elevate it above random, coarse, and abusive treatment: the holy is whatever cannot be safely profaned. Sacrilege, on the other hand, is an assault upon the sacred; and it can be either deliberate or accidental, and conscious or unconscious. Profanation is a matter of policy: it aims at dirtying something seriously held to be pure. Such a policy does not presuppose that nothing is holy. It does presuppose that something reserved as sacred is not holy. So one might seriously believe that something really holy has in fact been profaned by a religious insistence that it is sacred; and thereafter one might devote great energy and skill to attacking that barrier in the hope that the holy might come into its own. If, that is, one believed that sexuality were holy, one might attack the sacred institutions that have effectively made it dirty and/or trite. And if one believed that freedom were holy, one might well feel inspired to attack the sacred institutions that have effectively corrupted it. Thus the sacred emerges as that which men have arbitrarily demarcated as exempt from judgment and change, and thereafter have used to protect a stake demonstrably narrower than the common good of mankind.

Secularity liberates man from bondage to the sacred, and thus permits and encourages him to find the holy where and as he pleases or must. It tends therefore to make religion diffuse and idiosyncratic. Free to range beyond the precincts of the sacred, where might one turn next to find and grasp the holy? Prophecy is in order, but not prediction.

Six: a profound and powerful tension between the daily world and ecstasy. If the secular spirit has succeeded in generalizing the holy beyond the arbitrary limitations of the sacred, it has in that scored an ambiguous victory. For suppose that the pursuit of the holy is felt to be necessarily ecstatic. Who can tell how far beyond the boundaries of the daily world one may be carried by the power of the holy? Yet secularity operates effectively as such only upon the basis of images and concepts of a bounded and normal world, even though the boundaries are no longer fixed by divine fiat. Wherein then is its victory if, by fair means or foul, souls aspiring for largeness and vividness of life break free of those putatively humane limits?

We come thus upon a human phenomenon with which religious systems have been contending throughout history; and if the secularist learns nothing from this encounter let him blame no one but himself. This is the phenomenon of self-transcendence, the inextirpable human urge to break beyond the boundaries of self and self-reflecting world into a unity, power, and beauty unattainable in the daily world and thus inexpressible in its terms.

This human phenomenon prompts grave questions of a theological order, whatever the religious dispositions of the theologian. I propose now to state and consider some of those theological questions. They all have to do with a singular fact; namely, that man is obliged to put together powerful presentments of three worlds, and in a way that does not permit any of the three to block access to the others. But here surely is a great mystery: Each of the worlds presses upon the individual spirit the great benefits of routinization, but each hints of ecstasies to break past the routines of the others.

IV

The three worlds that lay unavoidable claims upon human life are:

> The daily world (Q, for quotidian)
> The world of nature (N)
> The ideal world (I)

We have therefore two prime questions about man's relation to any or all of these worlds:

> What mode of human transcendence is
> proper to each of them? (1)

How ought the Christian construe God's
transcendence in relation to each
of the worlds? (2)

The proper pursuit of these questions requires initial
clarity in the identification of the plural worlds. So this
is the immediate task.

Q is the world that claims us in that set of standard
beliefs, dispositions, attitudes, and overt gestures invoked
by reference to what everybody knows, believes, hopes,
and does. It is thus a commonsensical system: its values
are prima facie, its truths are taken for granted. It is what
claims us again when ecstasy is over. It is that state of
affairs in which we do not need merely to guess at how
work, play, and love will be appraised, for its rewards
and punishments are not reserved for eschatological
disclosure.

Q cannot help but put a high value on stability of
social structure and individual character, and upon instrumental intelligence and prudential wisdom. The Q component in human life is dedicated to keeping the show
on the road, keeping the store open, making do, getting
by, hoping to recoup tomorrow today's losses. It is the
world in which discretion is the better part of valor, but
it knows how to reward valorous defense of itself.

N is the world upon whose routines Q tries to establish
its own, for otherwise the human does not emerge in its
own right at all. Thus, man must eat to live: that is a law
of N. But in order to live he ought not to eat his brother:
that is a law of Q. If a man is starving he may obey N
rather than Q, but he might not, too; and thus in critical
cases Q and N jostle each other a good deal. But Q is
aware of the pressure from N, and N probably does not
care.

Thus the genetic code is nature's business. Man is learning very rapidly how to butt into that business—on pur-

pose, that is, both to learn how it works and to improve his situation, rather than blindly to change it and be changed by it. But beyond all such explorations, appropriations, and explanations there is an ongoing show in which man plays a very small role, and in which there is nothing or no one to remember him when his brief and uncertain day is done.

So Q and N intersect only so far as Q is disposed or required to do so for its own sustenance. Q is essentially teleological: if the orders and powers of the daily world fail to execute their particular purposes, they are modified and even abrogated. N is not so patently teleological. To know about N is a great human interest, fertilized by access to the ideal world (I). We do not know that N gives a fig for that itch. One can of course say that a cognitive appetite is the read-off of certain genes. I doubt that anything could be a clearer case of the pathetic fallacy than to ascribe to some genes a desire to learn about the rest.

The ideal world (I) overarches Q. The relations of I to N are essentially problematical. I includes both the possible and the desirable, the not-yet and the ought-to-be. There is a simple difference between these, so far as "X may very well happen" is plainly different from "I hope to God X never happens."

I overarches Q, and it may in some feature or other pervade Q as well. For Q is among other things a system of expectations, both great and small. England expects every man to do his duty through hell and high water. It is expected that you will pay your taxes. Thus the inevitabilities of Q: death and taxes. But one can renege on both, up to a point, and with warrants drawn on I. An individual can refuse to do his manifest duty and say a higher duty supports his refusal. So also for taxes. As for N: if he is properly shot for shirking his duty, he will die. This is nothing to N—from dust to dust, and the commotion in between is of no concern. But it matters greatly to Q. Fundamental challenge to its fundamental routines cannot be ignored.

Nonetheless, fundamental challenges of Q are inspired by access to I. The daily world is open to all kinds of criticisms that go beyond the working assumptions of Q and that may in fact put those assumptions under direct fire.

But N can also be reached by I through the mediation of man. Obedient to a vision of a good—or at least a better—society, men may decide to use natural resources in a way different from the routines of Q but yet compatible with some of Q. But does I make any difference to N when man is not around? Is N itself somehow obedient to I? Or is I by itself (that is, taken in abstraction) without life?

Such questions lure us out on the deeps of metaphysics and religion. We are not ready for that trip, though we are nudged toward the depths whensoever we properly consider the readiness of Q to justify itself in its relations to N and to itself by appealing to I. But also to justify itself to God.

Q's appeal to I in order to checkmate individual access to I (or for that matter, to God) is a good point at which to ask the first of the theological questions mentioned above. This is one of the important ways in which Q is (and not simply employs) a system for routinizing human self-transcendence. The ecstatic breakaway from Q into I is a formidable possibility at every moment in the life of Q, for there is no telling when doubt about the finality of Q's routines will ascend into sublime certainty that Q is the shabbiest of lies rather than a systematic and fitfully benign illusion. There is nothing for it then but for Q to insist that everything in I pertinent to the ordering of human life is already available in Q. This can be brought off with a fair measure of philosophic subtlety, as follows.

Perhaps I is not a world at all but is the product of human imagination and need, and is therefore to be grounded in Q. Surely men tend to imagine that the inadequacies of their Q could be relieved if all agreed now to do such-and-so. But there is precious little uniformity in what they thus imagine, partly because Q worlds suffer from a very wide range of inadequacies, and partly because men draw upon I for all sorts of remedies. Moreover, Q and I are really one world, for I is a set of idealizations of Q, and Q is a systematic response to the demands of I. So I supplies cues and directives for the ordering of Q, given the actualities of N.

It would seem to follow that I is nothing in itself, or is at best the invention of philosophers who are not quite able to cope with Q.

This sort of effort to corral human self-transcending in the direction of I is now in woeful disrepair. Given the very wide diffusion of Freudian and Marxian theologies, this is a very curious situation indeed. One is tempted to believe that the very success of these secularizing theologies has driven the most sensitive spirits into the idealistic ecstasy. But surely there are other telling factors in this crisis of secularity. One of these is the merciless pressure of that dimension of I called the not-yet.

Here again Q puts on a brave face, for Q cannot endure unless its constituents believe that it is an effective time binder. Here is the only history that matters and here is the route to the future. Or put it this way: Q cannot get away with its claims upon human energies and loyalties unless it advertises a successful administration of death as well as of life. This does not mean that death is the prime case of the not-yet. It does mean that every routinization of expectation in and as Q is already an awkward acknowledgment of death, death for the individual and for this Q and for all Q's. Thus the Q in which we live cannot yet make up its mind about the legal taking of life. Death still lingers as an instrument of policy, but the traditional theological-ethical appeals to the common good of mankind as a justification for such an instrument are now more than faintly tinged with desperation and with other elements of bad faith.

The idealistic ecstasy is not the only way out of Q. Even now it shares the stage with the naturalistic ecstasy. This requires some device for releasing biological vitalities, a device that momentarily suppresses individuality and personality and lets life flow in primordial unity and potency. Here the end in view is, paradoxically perhaps, to overcome the teleological system of society-and-self and escape at once the niggling erosions of Q and the relentless pressure of the not-yet.

So where the idealistic ecstasy counsels, "Become what you ought!" the naturalistic ecstasy counsels, "Throw off the criminal restraints of Q and I, and simply enjoy!"

How then is the loyal inhabitant of Q, antecedently convinced that Q is enough for his life, to thread his way among the options in a time when nothing about Q is more uncertain than its capability for making a coherent routine out of the thrust for self-transcendence? The problem goes from strength to strength; and the tranquility of Q is shattered into the predictable future.

Yet the very existence of Q is an achievement of human transcendence vis-à-vis N, the world of nature. Powerful philosophical minds in the modern world have sought to resituate man in the bosom of Nature, partly in reaction to the idealistic absorption of Nature into Spirit, and partly in positive response to the astonishing scientific triumphs of evolutionism. Nature thus celebrated is not the affair of ordinary experience. It is just as certainly not the value-free affair that emerges from scientific treatment of ordinary experience. The Nature of naturalistic philosophical evocation lures man—construed as being far more plastic than classical metaphysics could allow— into creativity marvelously harmonious with the inarticulate powers of life elsewhere in the cosmos.

But, again, this is not the feel of the nature with which Q man must contend. Indeed the Q world is at best an uneasy truce with N. Q is an achievement of human creativity too. It is a system of make-do in the face of N. And even where the public face of N is bland and smiling all the day there are still the formidable powers of the night, and death is not friendly.

Nevertheless man's access to I, the ideal world, does not let him take even the greatest triumphs of Q as final. If, for the sake of Q, N in us must be sublimated, Q itself must yield to the pressure of the ideal. For no Q is sufficiently humane. In every Q, precious things must be sold off to keep the days moving in steady, sensible procession. Thus Q inevitably comes to prize routine quite as much as N and has no greater success than momentarily convincing us that its routines are really a matter of "doing what comes naturally."

It would seem, then, that I is the transcending world itself, and is not itself meaningfully or creatively transcended. What higher ecstasy could be portrayed than union with the ideal world: no longer to perceive it dimly and from a great distance, but at last to be in it as what one ought to be, *sub specie aeternitatis.*

The perennial attractiveness of this notion testifies to persistent ambiguities in the concept of transcendence, some of which we have already reviewed. The severest difficulty with the view is not, however, any of its ambiguities. Rather, it is its distrust of the actual, of which Q is but one formation, and one object of suspicion. For the actual is a break in the chain of ideal necessity; it stinks of contingency, not only of the "It might have been otherwise," but also of "Who knows how it will turn out?"

Thus, actuality has its own mode of transcendence vis-à-vis I. Whatever is actual has a solidity of being in principle denied I. This solidity of being is the joy of all desiring in Q. Q is trying to be actual, in other words.

This is its peculiar glory and its peculiar wretchedness as well. But even in the depths of its misery it is better off than I, because I has no power in its own right at all. I can claim but it cannot enforce. Q can enforce, and it is always being tempted to identify this power as the essence of rightful claim, which it is not.

But we must not overlook the fact that the actual is an individual rather than a system or an order. This is the seat of Q's wretchedness, since Q is a system. System is something created by actual individuals as an extension and/or synthesis of their powers. Thus Q has about it a remarkable illusion; namely, that there is no meaningful life outside it, whereas in fact the actual individual is already outside it, so far as he is actual. As actual, he is already living into a future, a not-yet, about which Q can really do nothing better than to say, "Who knows what will happen?" Moreover, the actual individual is that, is actual, because he is already a synthesis of existence and possibility, and of fact and value. The actual is a realization, the proper or essential fixity of which is a value rather than a fact. Fact is what has happened, and as such is forever immutable. But the actual is an aim-being-realized, a good being materialized. Upon this process I impinges only through the envisagements of actual individuals. N is there to receive the results. Q is the systematic minimal assessment of their value.

V

God is the supremely actual, the quintessentially individual. The key to his transcendence of all the worlds is thus to be found in his actuality.

As a human creation, Q is a tragicomic analogy of N as God's creation. Man is an artificer. So is the beaver, and the paper wasp. They build to protect themselves against nature: unfriendly elements and predators. Yet they are thoroughly situated in this same nature; they do not deny, hinder, or worship it. But man is the Q maker. He believes his creation partakes of divinity because it is a world, whereas beavers and wasps can boast only colonies.

Viewed theologically, there is no mystery about God's transcendence of any and all Q worlds. He is beyond any power to contain him that any or all Q's might boast. Indeed, he belongs to none of them; none is an object of particular divine concern. For if the human person as actual does not live either in or for a Q world, why should God?

As for N, it is God's creation. He is in it only so far as any artist is in his work. But this does not mean that N is best construed, theologically, as a flat, static, and thus uninteresting backdrop for some historical drama. Indeed not. Perhaps there is not life everywhere in the system of nature. But wherever there are actual individuals there is assuredly life: energy under the control of appetition, and appetition responsive to the good.

Thus again the tragicomic character of the Q world, for N itself is not all routine. God has not left it indifferent to chance and novelty. And if there are bloody enmities in it, none is predicated on the assumption that N is not big enough for all the warring species. Furthermore, so far as N is a living system at all, it is symbiotic, a harmonium of ends rather than irresolvable conflict.

I, the ideal world, must seem at first glance somehow dearer to God's life than any other world. Or have the idealistic ecstatics and metaphysicians misled us on this matter? They have, I think. What God, himself supremely actual, is after, is actuality; or, rather, actualizations. That is why Christians believe that man is created in God's image. But this does not mean that God seeks imitations— godlets, simulacra, repetitions. As actual, God is altogether disposed to the maximization of value. So far he may properly be said to depend upon ideality, even if it is a feature of his own being. In God, the tug of the ideal is the ultimate reconciliation of the ought-to-be and the might-be, the good and the possible. He is what the entire cosmic (and this includes the historical) process is struggling to become. In picture-language, God is out there in the future. This does not mean that he has already experienced what has not yet happened on earth or elsewhere in the affairs of actual beings. It means that God's envisagement of the good binds the entire cosmic process toward its realization.

VI

How then is God Transcendent, the supremely actual individual, related to human actuality? Here we return to the primordial Christian image of God: that being who binds himself to his creation for the fulfillment of its possibility.

"Man" is a name, not primarily of an ideal, however splendid, but of an actuality, a living synthesis of existence and ideality.

Thus man functions in rightly ordered human life as an ideal. The word "man" names a commonwealth not yet visible and palpable, a state of affairs that includes everything human and in which everything included is affirmed.

So identified, man is an inordinately harsh judgment upon any and every Q world. Every Q legislates exclusions, some of which are relative, and some absolute. In our Q, the poor are excluded from the promise and the instrumentalities of that self-improvement presumably at the heart of the American Dream. The black man is excluded from preferential living districts. But it is a tender part of the American theology to believe that no one is absolutely excluded from some of the proper benefits of this society. Yet we license the killing of capital offenders against this society. That is a fair example of an absolute exclusion. Belief in a divine everlasting punishment is another one.

God intends the overcoming of all exclusivist structures and principles. That is why we say that no Q is an object of particular divine concern, except in the sense of God's unalterable opposition to anything that hinders the flow of human life outward and upward into the commonwealth of man.

Thus, God pledges his full support for every human aspiration to that commonwealth. But here God seems to be confronted with a choice: identifying with human individuals seeking to find themselves in love of others; or lifting human life bodily, so to speak, into his own life.

The proper novelty of the Christian view of God Transcendent is a settled determination to allow God to have it both ways. For the Christian believes that God is in Jesus Christ and Jesus Christ is God fully present to and with human beings. And the Christian believes that man is thus actualized as a member of the divine community. God is beginning and end; but in the end he is not by himself but has fellowship with man.

Human self-transcendence, therefore, in the Christian view is aimed at God. This is in no way a program or design for escaping from the world if by "world" one means the human condition in space and time, fully exposed at once to the vicissitudes of life in N and the temptations of life in Q. Since the aim of man's self-transcendence is God, any significant achievement in that line is an acquisition of power to love the world as it ought to be loved; that is, passionately and wisely. Inevitably, therefore, the Christian life from its historical beginnings is construed as ministry to the world, looking toward the reconciliation of man to God and thus of men to man.

So it is the case that for the Christian the secondary aim of self-transcendence is the human commonwealth, man. We say "secondary" simply because in the Christian view one is not entitled to live for man unless first he lives to God, and not because man comes limping into the purview of the Christian only after he has said his prayers and put down his bets—hopefully in that sequence. But let us also be clear that this sense of the priorities, God first and then man, is not the product of piety alone or perhaps even primarily. There is behind it some reflection upon human history: for in that tale man has often been loved and indeed served with ferocious ardor while actual human beings perished aforetime both for want of attention and from the unconscionable cruelty of fanatical visionaries. Thus both from history and the gospel the Christian may learn that man must descend from the I world, the realm of ideality, into the material circumstances of some Q world, in order to be perceived rightly and rightly loved. For love is richest and best when it goes out to and returns from an actual being, and there is no actual human being accessible to the normalities of intercourse who is not an inhabitant of some Q world.

But right here a momentous problem arises. If it is the case that the actual person lives beyond any and every Q by virtue of being actual, why is the typical encounter of person with person so deeply embedded in Q and bounded by Q's perimeters? For that is surely the feel of the matter. We seem therefore to be hounded all the way home by an astonishing paradox: it is in Q's best interests to make its people feel at home in it; yet, at least in our Q, "we are strangers when we meet." In fact our Q seems to be dedicated, insanely, to maximizing and generalizing alienation to its furthermost limits.

Again I must leave to the social scientist the task of tracing the kinds and magnitudes of alienation in this society. Here let me ask, rather, whether the rapid instrumentalizing of human life is not a prime cause of the paradoxical disquietude at the heart of Q. I believe this is the case. If it is the case, then any secularist gospel that celebrates some world as enough for any legitimate human aspiration had better be swift to identify what world that is. Surely the Q world is a very poor candidate for that election, if it is the case that the primacy of the use value of human life is our Q's contribution to the human commonwealth.

The truth about this Q may not be that bleak. We should hope that it is not, but we should not let hope blind us to the truth, whatever it is. In any case there is enough to be done to bring the standard levels of aspiration in this Q up to the requirements of actuality. It is not given to Q to redeem itself, but the actual agents living in it can certainly make it more responsive to the essential demands of man. This they can do only so far as they see God and resolutely obey him.

VII

Ecstatic breakaway from this Q of ours seems daily to become a strict necessity for more and more of Q's denizens. One of the accidental wonders of the technological society is the splendid proliferation of materials and techniques for ecstasy. Mankind has long possessed a variety of means for lowering consciousness to the vanishing point, and this immemorial lore of narcosis is remarkably similar to the practice of death. But now our Q seems quite as interested in consciousness-expanding ecstasy: the augmenting, rather than the diminishing, of human power. (This rather nicely exemplifies the profound ambiguity of freedom in this world—the flight from the arbitrary confinements of existence, and the flight toward actuality.)

The traditional religious communities still extant in our Q world are predictably suspicious of all but the tamest ecstasies. This may be explained as so many expressions of a maternal concern for the well-being of Q. The concern and the suspicions may quite as well be misplaced and exaggerated, for the great mother of ecstasy is religion. Unhappily, our Q world may have become so preoccupied with religion as a powerful instrument of social control that religion as a disciplined ecstatic opening to God is concealed behind a dark cloud of suspicion. If this is the case, the Christian—church and individual—has a great and taxing work to do. For God in Jesus Christ draws all mankind into his own actuality. Therefore each human being is destined to be raptured out of the definition any normal synthesis of I and N and Q can achieve for him. And it will not do, for this divine purpose, to seek to postpone that ecstatic union with God until some final moment of the world-historical process. Upon whomever it dawns that this is the acceptable year of the Lord (and this as something incomparably richer and more powerful than an interesting item for belief), it will surely break in as ecstasy, as a pulling away from the roots and the boundaries of the normal world. When God, supremely and everlastingly actual, speaks as and for himself, what is really possible for man and therefore what is really desirable for us comes wonderfully into sight and sound and touch, and the normal world retires into its proper magnitude. It is after all something men have made. If it does not properly serve man it cannot in any way glorify God.

VIII

There is very little empirical indication that the spirit of secularity is forging ahead without the benefits of religion or at least of religiousness. To be sure, prophets of the new age, or of the great tomorrow, look forward with longing almost too great to be borne to the time when man can at last live in, for, and through himself. Since we are not there yet, and I think nowhere near it, the question remains whether there is religion that provides an opening toward God Transcendent, that being who cares infinitely about the fulfillment of man in actual persons.

Wherever Christians, individually and corporately, do not live in that faith, they are missing the point. Secularity at its best is an eloquent plea for the commonwealth of man. As such it is a powerful rebuke to Christians living in bad faith. But the proper response to such a rebuke is not to abandon the Christian faith. It would be better to practice it.

Epilogue —
Theology in a New Key

THE THEOLOGICAL ENTERPRISE consists of an ongoing process in which elements from the past are juxtaposed by and collide with elements in the contemporary context. Our age experiences the tension between the juxtaposition and the collision in an agony that has shaken the beliefs of a large number of Christians and that has brought one community after another to the verge of schism and hatred.

But theology can be the adventure of creating a new vision that is integrative for an age that is at a loss at many points. Sometimes I stand at the open sea and wonder if we have failed entirely: despite Auschwitz and Hiroshima, we have not learned; the ghettoes are in revolt, and the hope of peace is surely not at hand. In the church, people scold the leaders for their confusion. Perhaps a book on the problem of secularity and secularism has a place for a personal theological statement. I simply intend to juxtapose, by way of experiment, certain Biblical passages with certain contemporary experiences and I shall try to show what they mean to me and what I think they ought to mean to theology. I believe that much human creativity results from such experimentation.

These pages will not contain exegesis of any kind. Nor will they give any specific formulas. Ours is an epoch that has discovered the tentativeness of all our statements and it would be a mistake to present answers when what I

Previously unpublished.

have are certain directions in which to seek answers. What is more important to me than the actual answers is the possibility of suggesting a common ground on which the problems could be debated by some of us who represent new directions in theological thinking. I do not count myself as part of the "God is dead" theology—what a confused term! Nor do I want to use the phrase "radical theology," although I like it. It would be presumptuous to use this word for our age alone, since every creative theological attempt in Christian tradition was radical in its time, from Valentinus to Nicaea to Abelard and Luther. Only in retrospect does what was radical turn into comfortable security. As these pages will show, I do not like the word "secular" either, since I do not believe there is a substantive difference between the sacred and the secular. Instead, I would prefer the phrase "Theology in a New Key," even though what I present is at best a series of experimental suggestions that the reader may use to create his own new vision.

CREATION AND THE EXPERIENCE OF A NEW COSMIC VISION

I begin my case by contrasting the stories about the creation of the world in the beginning of the book of Genesis with our present-day space experiences. Every first-year student of the Old Testament learns that the Bible starts out with two different mythic accounts of creation:

Myth I: Genesis 2:4b–25
Myth II: Genesis 1:1 to 2:4a

Myth I is the older one, originating in a half-nomadic, early agrarian culture that had little knowledge of the universe and of life's evolution. From the dust of the earth man was created; he was given animals and vegetation as "his far more pleasant garden," and out of his ribs came the woman whom Milton called "simplicity and spotless innocence." The people who originally created this mythic tale experienced life on the precarious border of the desert. When rain fell on the arid land the earth became a garden. Myth II arose from very different cultural views: influenced by the discoveries of Mesopotamian astronomers and formed at a much more advanced stage of Hebrew culture, it portrays the creation of the universe as a cosmic drama, beginning with the evocation of light, leading through the creation of the sun, the moon, and the stars to plants, to the lower and higher animals, and finally to man. Myth II understands the creation of life as a sequential process and thereby reveals a growing sophistication of human insight into the nature of life, almost a prelude to modern evolutionary explanations.

It is astonishing at first sight that the redactor of the book of Genesis dared to combine these stories, so far apart from each other in the worlds they express and in the images they mean to convey. The two myths are incompatible at many points. The redactor of Genesis who put them next to each other did not realize that in so doing he was exhibiting the kind of tension that comes along inevitably with the historical process. This type of uncritical juxtaposition of historical fragments has been going on since man became a historical being. It is only with our recently developed historical sensibilities that we have become *conscious,* as earlier ages were not, of history as a process of accretion, modification, adaptation, and rejection.

The two Genesis myths reveal this dynamic. Both speak about the same thing: the act of creation and its culmination in the appearance of man. But the myths also disagree. The order of creation differs radically; in one it goes from man to plants to animals to the woman, in the other from light through different stages of plants and animals to the simultaneous creation of man and woman. In the older tale, the woman was seen as part of man, as his possession; in the later tale, she is his equal partner,

at least potentially. The world in which the first myth
takes place is that of a tribal plain, flat dry land that blos-
soms when rain begins to fall; the world of the second
includes a domed firmament above the earth. The juxtaposition of the two stories creates a tension that makes
the reader feel both the ties with and the break from the
world portrayed by the earlier story. The two myths prove
how grossly mistaken the scholar is when he imagines
the Bible to contain a single cosmic vision or one experience of life. At the very outset of the book of Genesis,
the dynamism of human experience is demonstrated.

Since Genesis was assembled, man has found himself
having to cope with one world view after another.
Twentieth-century man's most revolutionary experience
of this changing perspective is his adventure and risk into
space. It is this awareness and experience of space which
I want to juxtapose to the two Biblical accounts, as Gen.,
ch. 1, was juxtaposed to Gen., ch. 2. On a brilliant night
outside a cabin high up in the Alps I saw for the first
time with my naked eyes the Andromeda nebula. With
my companions I set out to climb one of the icy peaks.
Gradually the dazzling morning light displaced the stars,
and at the first rest stop we reckoned that in the two
hours we had climbed the light of the giant nebula had
traveled more than a billion miles. This distance, vast to
our imagination, is actually miniscule: the light had left
its source one million and a half years before. When these
rays from Andromeda started toward us, we were not yet.
Man was not yet come. It was during the immense journey
of that light that man appeared; and only at the very
last moment of that journey, in the last half of 1 percent
of the distance, did our history take place.

There is a second experience, more radical even than
this, which I also mean to place beside the myths of
Genesis: the experience captured in the beautiful view
of the earth that the astronauts photographed across the
desert of the moon. There we were, there was our planet,

seen from outside, a bluish-marble globe with its white clouds and red-tinged continents, rotating in the dark emptiness of the universe, so precariously alone, so beautifully unique. Of course we have known for a long time that we spin precariously in space. The scientists of Alexandria found it out in antiquity, Copernicus knew it, Brecht wrote a play, *Galileo,* that reminds us of it. But whoever is sensitive to the growth and development of the human person knows of the crucial difference between the stage in which we simply know and the stage in which we confirm what we know by feeling and seeing. For the first time in the history of our planet we *saw* what the astronomers had taught us. We *saw* ourselves spinning in space and verified with our eyes what our minds had imagined. Through the immediacy of the photograph and the television screen, space became tangible, and penetrated our consciousness with new concreteness. The recent space explorations, above all the Apollo adventure, brought the dimension of space from the sphere of cerebral knowledge into the sphere of total human experience.

Why do I juxtapose these particular cosmic images? There are many others, of course, that I could cite from ancient and from more recent periods. But a comparison between the world consciousness in Genesis and our own spatial awareness has special pertinence to the contemporary theological task. Certain dimensions in them are constant. Man looks out into the world around him, into the garden beside the desert, into the heavens, into the universe. He wants to find out where he is, not only in order to find his place in life and his relation to the past, but also in order to go on. So he inquires into the mystery and turns what he learns into a story, and that story reflects the way he experiences the world around him. He creates because he experiences; yet, equally important, his creativity in turn enriches his awareness and enables him to experience in a deeper way. This circularity can only be partially analyzed. Like the people who created and transmitted the two myths on the creation of man, we look astonished at the world in which we find ourselves, and out of a mixture of poetry, history, and science we create in turn a new vision of life. It is that vision which I call theology.

The crucial change from the world consciousness behind the creation of the Genesis myths to that behind the contemporary space experience lies in a conceptual shift from an enclosed to an open universe. One hears frequently that the change lies in the replacement of a vertical construction of life by a horizontal one, the historical continuum. But that is not the problem of contemporary theology, since that change began in antiquity, and both the Christian church as political institution and Christian theology as an attempt to clarify the early Christian models of incarnation, atonement, resurrection, and Parousia actually developed within the tension between the vertical and the historical. Pertinent to contemporary theology in respect to the space experience is a more radical tension. To put it in personal terms, I find myself not only a historical being, caught by and creating within the evolutionary process of history, but I also find myself in an empty universe, on a planet that has been rotating around the sun for billions of years. In this situation I feel myself part of the cosmic rhythm by which the axis of the earth turns only once every 25,000 years and by which our galaxy turns once in perhaps a million years. It is not merely that the vertical has been replaced by or juxtaposed to the horizontal but that both the vertical and the horizontal have been put in tension with the dimension of space, and this means with rotation, rhythm, gravity, and relativity.

I want to give an example of this change from the field of church architecture. One of the typical buildings appearing time and again in the history of the church was the cruciform structure, a central space with a vaulting, domelike ceiling; for example, San Vitale, Hagia Sophia,

Aachen, and Michelangelo's St. Peter's. The mosaic of
Galla Placidia consists of a starry canopy set in the domed
ceiling above the central space of the sanctuary. These
domes express visually the world view of Myth II. Even
the Romanesque and Gothic interiors represent either
rounded or vaulted spaces reminiscent of or symbolic of
heaven. However, when Le Corbusier built his church
at Ronchamp a new kind of symbolism appeared. To be
sure, in some ways this church still seems to imitate the
idea of a medieval fortress, perhaps transformed into a
bunker of the Maginot Line, and one can see in the contours of the concrete structures images of a cave or of
a ship. Yet the walls and roofs also express something
radically different. They are concave, they seem to move,
the roof is floating. Traditional symmetry is replaced by a
dynamic flow. There is a fascinating mathematical character to this building. The numerous irregular windows
are not chaotically cut into the curving wall, but are har-
monized by the geometric law of the golden mean, applied not in any static or symmetric proportionality from
a given axis, but in a relationship that suggests freedom
in motion. The step from the Romanesque cathedral of
Périgueux to the church of Ronchamp reflects the changes
in our perception of the cosmos to experiencing a dynamic open universe.

I can also illustrate the change by pointing to a small
Episcopal church, which William P. Wenzler built in
Elmgrove, outside Milwaukee. This hyperbolic parabola
is clearly no longer definable in terms of the tension between the vertical universe and the historical consciousness of man. The roof, actually the entire building, seems
to take off from the earth, toward the skies, forward and
upward in a motion that contains the tension between
rotation and gravity and reminds us of the jet taking off,
and of the space capsule hurtling around the globe. To be
sure, as one enters the church many traditional elements,
liturgical as well as social, can be found, just as in all of

our lives strata of the past are in tension with the new. Yet the impact of Wenzler's building lies in its radical expression of the new awareness of space our century has brought us in the years from the first flight of the brothers Wright to man's first landing on the surface of the moon.

To take account of these changes is a first prerequisite to a new theological task. The vertical axis of the dome and the horizontal security of a stable earth created a whole framework of religious language, the categories of up and down, heaven and hell, the New Jerusalem, the saving act of the past. To many a frightened Christian, the claim that these traditional language models are no longer speaking to our age seems almost synonymous with announcing the termination of Christianity and civilization altogether. To be sure, the discarding of vertical metaphoric speech in ritual, prayer, church order, and metaphysic has contributed to the turmoil of our age. To many, law and order are unthinkable without vertical concepts to support them. I am not afraid. I believe that out of the new spatial consciousness, no less than out of our historical consciousness, models will emerge that will make it possible for us not only to function passably but to live with renewed hope and a new kind of affirmation. The remaining pages of this chapter will try to outline the directions in which I personally see signs of such a new vision. One thing I know: the next generation will have to try to establish language models that arise from a conscious grappling with the new spatial awareness in us, so that we can deal more pertinently and more imaginatively with our contemporary experiences.

Does the development which I have outlined necessarily imply a total secularization of the church? I do not think so. The step from the tribal world in myth I to the dome in myth II to the cosmic vastness we sense as we compare ourselves with the Andromeda light to the photos of ourselves televised back from the contours of the moon is not inevitably a movement toward growing secularity.

It is rather an expanding world awareness with profound implications for the religious life, a world awareness that demands new relations not only between man and the universe but between man and society, which religions must begin to take into account. For the replacement of a stable axis by a dynamic motion is a development neither toward nor away from secular patterns. It is related to the problem of secularity for social reasons. A religious group tends to identify with a certain vision of the world. When this vision is challenged or begins to erode, the group feels its identity slipping and then labels the challenge disparagingly as secularization. It feels its social, liturgical, ethical, and theological presuppositions threatened by the historical evolution.

To give another example: To some profound believers at the exile, the world of myth II, so traditionally religious to us, might have appeared to be a terribly secular vision of life compared to the safe world with which they could identify in myth I, and the courage of the redactor to incorporate myth II into the opening of the book of Genesis may have been as radical as juxtaposing our four-dimensional universe to the beautifully enclosed dome of Hagia Sophia. Only because we have blurred, as for instance in the frescoes of the Sistine Chapel, the two stories of creation as if they were one vision do we fail to remark any more the contradictoriness of the creation myths in the Bible. The experience of seeing the Andromeda nebula and of admiring the photographs of the astronauts may look to a later generation like examples of a safe, nonsecular vision of life compared to their own new images and visions.

Changes in awareness and consciousness do not come overnight, of course. We carry along rudiments of the past, and in ages of transition the world of the past is closely intertwined with new insights that are opening up. The world of *Paradise Lost* fascinatingly intermingled various interpretations of Genesis: the world dangling on a pendulum, and the new emerging world consciousness of the Copernican age. In this my city of Philadelphia, the man thinking in terms of quantum mechanics and the cycles of the universe finds himself a few blocks from people believing in the "evil eye" or practicing voodoo; more than this, the same man, while living in one part of his life as an advanced inquirer into the most contemporary secrets of life, on another level might participate in extremely archaic religious or pseudoreligious groups. The scientist may be a hard-core, pre-Vatican II Roman Catholic, or a fundamentalist, or a member of a Masonic lodge. The lives of all of us are marked by such inconsistencies of attitude and development. So when I talk about finding certain new theological images and life patterns I do not mean that the earlier ones can be eliminated magically. No human being replaces his past overnight. I do claim, however, that it is our task to respond positively in our inquiry, from the Christian tradition out of which we live, to the challenge of new spatial experiences.

I do not care if the new spatial awareness is given the sacred or the secular label, but I must cope with the fact that we have entered a new stage of that "untravel'd world whose margin fades Forever and forever when I move."

Ex., CH. 3, AND THE HISTORICAL CONSCIOUSNESS

Let me put a second Biblical story beside certain contemporary events. One of the most impressive historical tales is that of the exodus. The basic event of the exodus cycle is God's calling Moses in the third chapter of the book of Exodus. Moses, tending his flock, sees the flaming bush and reverently takes his shoes off to hear the revelation of Yahweh: the command to lead Israel out of Egypt. For Jewish life, the story has always had a fundamental significance; in Christian tradition it has been painted and sung about and employed, as in neo-orthodox theology, as the Christian view of history and salvation.

The story seems to offer an absolutely clear-cut solution to a historical dilemma. God wanted his people out of Egypt, and Moses received his direct, unambiguous command to lead them. We have no such resources of mythic belief in divine authority for our difficult communal decisions. The United States has been torn apart because of the divided opinion on the war in Southeast Asia. In the elections of 1964 and 1968 the two major parties, caught in that dissension, intensified by the brutality of the war itself, practically committed political suicide. They would give a great deal for a divine oracle to proclaim the direction we should take. But we have no such oracle. There is no theophany from the top of the Pentagon. Christian believers are no less divided on the war in Vietnam than those who do not share Christian convictions.

What makes things worse, there are not even guiding historical precedents. Many people have declared the British surrender at Munich in 1938 to be the disastrous event leading to the horrors of World War II. Some people see a direct parallel to Vietnam: just as it was a tragic error to give in to Hitler at Munich, it would be a mistake to give in to Ho Chi Minh. Other people say that the situation of Munich is not the situation of Saigon. In other words, there is no fixity in our positions. The relationship between principles and situations is neither constant nor absolute, but fluid. I have friends, for instance, who are absolute pacifists in the matter of Vietnam, but they are violently pro-Israel at the same time, defending Israeli military actions. Inconsistent, perhaps, but not absurd, because this kind of discriminate judgment arises out of a heightened awareness of the fluidity in the historical process. We have no one to call us to the burning bush and to tell us in that clear voice how to lead Israel out of South Vietnam—or out of Arab Palestine for that matter.

But was the historical situation so different for Moses? I would say not. The story of the burning bush was Israel's poetic tale about its own past, and not the report of an authentic miracle. To many readers this sounds like an obvious statement that has been seen by one part of Western culture for over two centuries; to others it sounds like a blasphemy. But I see no better way to go farther in our theological task than by acknowledging the fundamental fact: that a Biblical supernatural event is a people's poetry about its past. There were no sound waves from God reaching Moses' ears. We do not have to construct any theory to explain why the bush did not burn down. The situation of the Hebrew tribes in Egyptian slavery was no better than our situation is: they received no call, no oracle, no miracle. They had to make their decisions, they dared to break from slavery, they acted, and they also failed. The tale about a divine revelation was Israel's affirmation of its past; in the episode of the burning bush Israel created the poetic vision by which it tried to understand its history. The difference lies in the degree of our *awareness* that we are on our own.

This insight may look like a destructive act of tearing down the belief of entire traditions. But it is destructive only for those who still need the support of a mythic illusion, as if the myth were anything else but poetic vision. Actually the insight into such a story as a story about man's past can become exceedingly creative in several ways. It frees us from the chimera that we can rely on supernatural intervention in human affairs. Some people, even quite sensible ones, still hope so desperately for a new revelation that they are willing to take seriously the most bizarre preachers if they promise such a revelation. One day in a European train I saw a well-dressed woman across from me avidly reading a pamphlet about Father Divine in New York. As I began to question her I found out that she had never been in America and that she had absolutely no idea what Father Divine's Harlem movement was all about. But being dissatisfied with what she called the godless state of the church, she was simply looking for someone to give her a supernatural revelation. The difference between the woman in the European train and myself is not that I reject the mysterious and the marvelous in history. The difference lies in the fact that she expects the poetic models of the past to work literally in her life, while I can no longer accept a fusion of history and mythic poetry that fails to distinguish between what is possible and what is merely symbolic. To me the creation of Venice out of the Adriatic Sea and the conquest of space by man in the twentieth century are miracles no less spectacular than the exodus of the Hebrew tribes.

We must take into consideration, therefore, this profound difference between the realities of a historical situation as we have to live it in our daily lives, no matter how painful and tedious and frustrating they are, and the situation recorded as history by men writing after the event and adding to it mythic and poetic elements. Susanne Langer is quite correct: man is a symbol-making being. We need to create symbols in order to understand ourselves, and frequently we find these symbols in our past. Our poetic rendering of this past is therefore partly factual, partly symbolic. In the case of the burning bush episode, the tension between history and symbol must be clearly seen: some scholars are not sure if all the tribes were actually in Egypt; and the events of the exodus very likely took place quite differently from the descriptions in the Pentateuch. Furthermore, the description is in effect a poetic theophany created by the Hebrews not only to express their past but their present hopes as well. The Hebrew tribes *did* conquer Canaan, and they did establish a vital culture of their own. To look back to that time in the desert meant to find strength to deal with the present. The historical tale often serves this function: creating a perspective without which all day-to-day actions seem totally coincidental. When Israel's people created the theophany of Ex., ch. 3, they created a perspective from which their lives received meaning.

To understand the story of the burning bush as poetic

theophany is therefore to free oneself from the illusion of any supernatural intervention in the past, and to see the historical tale as a synthetic attempt to gain perspective, so that we can function and create in the present and find hope to go on. These two dimensions reveal the deep tension in our relation to the past of which I spoke in the discussion on the two Genesis myths. In the first place, we have become conscious of what we are doing; when we confront the need to decide about the war in East Asia, we can't go to the burning bush for an answer. In the second place, confronting the symbol-making creativity of the book of Exodus invites us to seek language models that are different in kind from those which the antique world used. Both of these are directly related to the issue of secularity.

To speak of the first, the problem of secularization of the mythic tale had already begun in the Old Testament. Robert Gordis recently claimed that the new trend toward secularism in Protestant thought and life is actually nothing else but Hebraizing Christianity. Although this interpretation ignores many vital aspects of this Protestant development, in one way I agree. The Old Testament was indeed in the process of secularizing its own mythological background. The book of Deuteronomy, for instance, closes with the statement that after Moses no prophet rose anymore who spoke directly with God. This sentence is an explicit acknowledgment that the Moses cycle with its miracles belongs to the past. Now the redactor of Deuteronomy who wrote this sentence down was surely not aware of how radical his statement was. Many hundred years after him, Origen made the same observation in regard to the New Testament when he said sadly that in the time of the apostles there were signs and miracles but in his own age there were not any more. Both of these insights prove how far back the demythologizing with which we are dealing today began. The difference between the redactor of Deuteronomy and Origen, on one side, and our present age is simply that we have become more conscious of the functional nature of myth. We *know* that man finds security and strength by being told of a theophany of the past, a miracle which he does not experience himself but which somehow he can believe in.

To speak to the second point, that the symbols which we create must be different in kind from the symbols of the past: The invasion of Normandy under General Eisenhower and the slaughter at Auschwitz have become symbols for our age. I listened as a boy to Churchill's speech about fighting to the end with blood, sweat, and tears, and that speech for many of us has become symbolic. In a way, Churchill's eloquent phrase has functioned for the war years the way the exodus tale functioned for Israel, with one exception: not only do we know that Churchill's words were part of the human drama and of the human risk which could have gone wrong, but we also realize that neither Churchill nor the contemporary poet would with any great likelihood create a story of supernatural intervention to explain the phenomenal British endurance in the air battle of 1940. A miracle it was, that air battle, not too different from the way the Hebrew tribes delivered themselves from the yoke of the Pharaohs. But the poetic story in which this event becomes a symbolic perspective for the present would not be a mythic tale but a novel, a poem, a vivid historical account or a drama.

There are two observations I must add to this analysis of Ex., ch. 3, and its symbolical implications for the present-day theology that will supply some perspective for contemporary man. I have made a case for viewing the mythological tradition critically and for searching for new symbolic language. I must reckon, however, not only with the fact that there are many symbolic traditions but that many segments of contemporary humanity are not willing to view the myth historically and consciously. A vast traditional religious world, from Protestant fundamentalism to orthodox Islam, is determined to hold fast to traditional models. Primitive religious experience is far from dying out. To mention only one example, the Rostopherians of Jamaica, a group which Leonard Barrett has analyzed. Furthermore, there is a whole search for non-symbolic expression of life, from Zen to the concrete poets of America. Only a certain percentage of people, even within the churches, will respond positively to attempts at theological experimentation. I have to be conscious of this fact. That does not mean, however, that I can be totally or uncritically open, but it does mean that I learn to distinguish the theological experiment from the crusade.

If it is true that even the past is not static but that we create the past by retaining certain elements of it only and rejecting others, then I must be prepared to believe the same fate is ahead for any perspective I evolve. Theology, Karl Barth used to say, must be rewritten every fifty years. Today it needs to be rewritten much more often, and frequently one writing runs into the next. While there is some despair in the face of the constant critique and the real danger of losing all certainty during the course of such rapid and interlacing developments, there is also real value in this state of affairs. This rapid criticism and reformation of perspectives can give to the theological enterprise the exciting character of experiment, an openness to the present that invites us constantly to search for the new.

ACTS, CH. 2, AND NEW FORMS OF COMMUNICATION

The second chapter of the book of The Acts displays a significant element of the early Christian process of expansion and communication. The author first describes the event of Pentecost and then puts into the mouth of Peter a sermon that is typical of the early Christian mode of communication. In this sermon the apostle proclaims the Christian salvation as a series of events beginning in the Old Testament, fulfilled in the life and death of Jesus of

Nazareth, and celebrated as occasion for thanksgiving in the Christian community. The media of this kerygma, which represented the missionary movement to both the Jew and the Gentile, were the written account and the spoken sermon. To be sure, the ancient church employed other media as well: the offering and eating of food and drink, and visual communication in its iconographic imagery and architectural forms. The ancient church grew because of the viability of these images, the myths behind them, and the force of its communal dynamic. Nevertheless the media of the written account and of the rhetorical presentation of faith in sermon, catechetical instruction, exhortation, and theological exposition are of pivotal importance to the growth of the ancient church. It is through these media that Christianity articulated itself: the passionate battles for an "authentic" faith, with constant repudiation of one group or another as "heretical," was largely waged by the media of the polemic sermon and the polemic written statement. What emerged was valid in Christianity for almost two millennia.

It is valid no longer. Our own age has devised dramatically new modes of communication so potentially *creative* as well as at times *coercive* that the very nature of Christian faith is bound to change radically. The authoritarian method of instruction in the faith is being challenged or at least supplemented by group processes that are essentially democratic. The seminar method on the university level is an example of one such group process. In the patristic age, in a homily on Acts, ch. 2, the bishop would instruct the faithful from his cathedra, giving the truth of the text; in the Protestant age, the minister preaching on Acts, ch. 2, from his pulpit delivered the Word; in the academic world, the professor of New Testament delivered lectures on the problems of Acts, ch. 2. In the seminar, however, an entirely new situation obtains, and a new type of learning experience takes place that modifies the purely cerebral faith-content of theology.

In the seminar, the process of teaching has become a process of learning, through which new insights and responses to the text can be creatively evolved. The meaning of the text no longer is a matter only of what the author intended or what the early Christian consciously understood in it, though both are important; in the seminar meaning is up for debate. Not only can different positions by scholars on Acts, ch. 2, be discussed, but the sharply divergent life experiences and attitudes of the discussants can meet in a dynamic interchange that perhaps reenacts or at least parallels the interactions of those who heard the text originally. Moreover, the discussants of the seminar interpret and apply the texts in ways relevant to their current lives. What the seminar does is an enactment of what happens when people confront history.

This process, exhibited in the example of seminar work, is directly related to the problem of secularity under discussion. For a large part of Christianity, what the church believed was determined by hierarchic leadership: in Catholicism by the bishop, the council, or the papacy; in Protestantism by the ministers and the various hierarchies of the denominations; in the universities by the professor at his desk. The sermon as well as the lecture and the encyclical reflect and belong to antique forms of authority and teaching. For many Christians the attempt to let the Christian individual participate seems synonymous with secularization. I would disagree if in such accusation secularization is construed only negatively. Rather, such participation can lead to a more productive relation between authority and community. The seminar requires not that the professor teach in the old sense, but that he confront history, or any other field for that matter, in company with his students. That does not imply an abdication of the task of teaching. In fact it is more demanding to allow free intellectual interplay in the classroom than to tell the students what to think. Of course the specialist on Acts, ch. 2, knows more than the students do, and should know a great deal more, being the expert who can offer valuable advice. But he is also one among others who learn. In this role he can actually communicate, with passion and conviction, his views on the text. But at the same time he may reveal his fears and his doubts. This kind of sharing may be as constructive in the growth and learning experience of the students, and of himself, as the mere communication of information. To be sure, this form of communal work contains the risk of undisciplined chatter, or of becoming nothing more than a therapy session. Obviously, universities as well as churches entering upon this type of interrelation must establish sensible safeguards against that.

An even more pervasive influence for change in Christian faith today is the proliferation of media incredibly different in kind from print and speech. Photography, film, radio, television: all mass media adding to ideas and events the dramatic immediacy of sound and sight in motion. On the way to her office the businesswoman hears the cruel statistics on Vietnam's casualties; in the living room families watch Biafran children starving to death; in both hemispheres sports fans follow the soccer championships by the millions; a whole nation watches the same nine o'clock movie on Friday night. These media bring the world closer to us. We have through them creative exposure to the plurality and openness of our planet as well as to its horrors. By them the individual's immediate relation to the world is intensified, as is his consciousness of being part of a whole. When the author of The Acts wrote his second chapter, he took for granted the Roman network of harbors, bridges, and roads, and the fact that his apostles could travel on this network, and that his opus on the expansion of the church could be sent throughout the empire to be read. Just as this assumption created in the early Christian the awareness of being part of the *catholica ecclesia*, the worldwide interchange possible through the new media furthers our world consciousness, our awareness of belonging to one humanity. This is true despite the negative possibility that such confrontations with other cultures can bring about fear reactions in the peoples of the world.

The two phenomena, the changed relationship in education and authority, and the new immediacy of communication, aggravate an old social problem by indiscriminately exposing people of various intellectual and emotional levels to ideas, images, conflicts, they may be unable to handle. Obviously, human beings develop at very different rates with different results. Each of us comes to terms with his own life and therefore confronts a text within the limitations of his own existential stage at any given moment. Some kind of insight into one's own behavior, for instance, can create permanent crisis, and a critical analysis of certain aspects of one's faith can destroy a person's identity.

One aspect of the danger can be illustrated in relation to the kind of critical confrontation without which no serious learning takes place. One can say with a great deal of probability that the event described in the beginning of Acts, ch. 2, did not take place, at least not as it is described and not with those results. The sermon that followed the event was not Peter's but was the product of the author of The Acts, patterned after many similar sermons given in his church, half a century after the event of Pentecost was said to have taken place. Some people are deeply hurt by this critical historiography, in the way some orthodox Jews would be hurt by a notion that Ex., ch. 3, does not speak about an actual communication between God and Moses, and in the way faithful Muslims would be incensed at the thought that the Koran could be seen in the same way I have examined the two myths of Genesis. Other people would employ all kinds of scholarly gimmicks in order to dispute such critical examination. But there are some who see in it a starting point for dealing with the text realistically. The plurality of reactions, which has to be taken seriously, does not eliminate the insight that there are developments that cannot be undone and that once we have become conscious of the fact that a myth is a myth we cannot return to the period in which we were not conscious of that fact. After all, there *is* change, and there *is* growth.

I mean no disparagement here to the young or to the uneducated; but I do have to make clear that the new learning processes, as well as the new media, do not free us from but rather aggravate the conflict of ideas present in the violent history of Christianity. Several years ago, a student of mine suddenly took up the practice of speaking in tongues, clearly a highly subjective emotional response to his religious search for experience. The sincerity of his conviction, supported by this very text in Acts, ch. 2, was unmistakable: it was for him a meaningful and absorbing experience of faith. One day after I had received a glowing letter from him, I happened to sit next to his bishop, who dismissed the whole matter contemptuously. He was obviously too "enlightened" to take this glossolalic foolishness of a young minister seriously and saw in it a potential danger to the social coherence of the church. Yet when I went on to verbalize my understanding of salvation and of the Pentecostal event as ancient man's search for meaning in life, he was equally dismissive of my "radical" understanding of the early church. We had all three been exposed to the primitive Christian text, but each was bound to a different response dictated by his particular emotional and intellectual frame of reference. The student clung to a literal acceptance; the bishop clung to liberalism; I opt for contemporary relevance.

Rev., ch. 21, and the Contemporary Social Revolution

Primitive Christianity believed in the Second Coming of Christ, in the New Jerusalem, and in the new heaven and the new earth. The New Jerusalem did not come, and the stars did not fall from the heavens. But the hope of radical change remained one of the strongest thrusts of Christianity throughout its tumultuous history. Eschatology is the poetry of social change, is antique science fiction in dramatic form, sometimes expressed in the primitive models of trumpets and golden doors and walls of jasper but more often translated into new secularized models. In the mosaics of S. Apollinare Nuovo, the port of Classe and the city of Ravenna are depicted as the locus of new life; in the town hall of Siena, Ambrogio Lorenzetti painted a medieval city as the model of good government; the Anabaptists hoped to establish the Kingdom of God in the city of Münster; the settlers of Massachusetts felt they were creating a New World.

Two things came together from the beginning in such hope for change. On one hand, Christianity identified with a certain place, a city, a land. On the other hand, this very city or land became itself the target of protest. Hoped-for change is always conceived in tension with what exists in the present. We can phrase the point differently. Christianity has frequently been a traditional religious force, i.e., a movement that offers psychological security and communal stability by cultic and mythic means. But it contains also in its basic drive the most poetic hope for change. Perhaps no other tension in Christianity is as painful and as creative as this one between cult and eschatology, a new version of the Old Testament conflict between religious needs served by the priests and the historical dynamic expressed by the prophets. The radical impetus to social change has been Christianity's most constructive contribution to the social dynamic. As Harvey Cox lately has expressed, the secular city of contemporary life is the place where the eschatological event is not simply a vision but is taking place and is expected to take place. In other words, we are conscious of vision as a social force that we can direct.

Our cities are aflame. The whites flee into the suburbs. The Negroes rebel against the ghetto in anger and frustration. Squad cars cruise day and night, and the students carry protest signs. For many, the secular city is Babylon rather than Jerusalem. However, the expanded perspective of history, and the enlargement of the human horizon by the explorations into space offer us valuable resources for meeting these problems. This chapter is not the place to develop a full-scale program outlining the role of theology in the urban chaos. But I should like to indicate what seem to me priorities.

To begin with, theology needs to make a contribution toward the transformation of the educational system. The present-day student rebellion is led frequently by irresponsible elements and it is quite possible that the unfortunate fascism employed in the tactics of the young will produce a backlash and delay the urgent changes for decades. But change must come. It is not just a matter of changing the curriculum of universities that still are dominated by Hellenistic rhetoric, medieval logic, Germanic scholarship, and Anglo-Saxon economics. Instead it is a matter of offering the young people a more meaningful educational process. The way to it is directly related to the kind of ideas in my remarks on new media and on the seminar. When people ask, What in the world has the student rebellion to do with the Christian tradition? I would have to answer, A great deal. Both the establishment of a medieval frame of philosophy and the coming of the Reformation were tied to students, and the reason for this connection is unmistakable: Christian theology, as the message of incarnation, of justification, speaks to the possibilities of man's self-renewal. The young generation asks in the most desperate way for a new humanity in a world it sees as utterly bizarre.

I want to point out one, perhaps the essential, factor in the need for change. The ancient educational process was a hierarchic one; the contemporary university or high school often is run in a hierarchic way, authoritarian, frequently like a corporation. The president is the boss of the institution, the chairman is the boss of the department, the professor is the boss of the class. When the students ask for a certain voice in the decision-making, they are not merely displaying juvenile arrogance and a drive for power but are reacting, intuitively perhaps, to the fact that the ancient hierarchic and hence also paternalistic models are being replaced by models of motion and rhythm. The process of finding new models is extremely painful and has produced one crisis after another. It could not be otherwise. But we are facing not the destruction of values —even though it looks like it—but a crying out for human relations in which the individual is permitted to be a responsible and integral part of society. Is this not a contemporary concretion of the beautiful image in patristic theology that God became man so that man could become divine?

The perspectives of history and of space can make a concrete contribution to the revolt that takes place in the ghetto. It sounds naïve and utopian today, but the need for racial reconciliation is perhaps the most urgent if not the most difficult of all contemporary needs. To be sure, we cannot on a page solve a problem that demands book after book and that splits America into warring factions. But we can say one thing: In the hundred thousands of years since man emerged on this lonely beautiful planet, the races have thus far lived in conflict and separation. The fact that in the American culture a meeting of the races is possible at all is hopeful. It is indeed an amazing phenomenon. We have streets and blocks and schools where the black and the white can meet. We are confronting in the racial rapprochement a change that is not going to be completed in a day, because it means a new experiment in human relationships. Last year two young people stood up after a lecture of mine and said: We have two years only to go and if the race issue is not solved in two

years it will be too late for the rest of history. The boys
were wrong. The great changes on this planet are not
solved over two years. This insight, to be sure, can serve
as a cheap escape by which we can excuse ourselves for
not doing anything at all. The insight, however, can also
lead to a strengthening of our hopes, and it is precisely the
reconciliation that comes out in day-to-day living, in
school and university, entertainment and politics, that
needs this kind of hope. To many, the thought that our
contribution to the next five centuries is so modest is
threatening. It does not need to be so.

The replacement of the vertical cosmological models by
those of rotation and rhythm is related to the racial conflict just as it is related to the revolt in the educational
enterprise. The hierarchic structure of society has often
dealt with the minority as with the lower stratum of man.
The Christian statement that "there is neither Jew nor
Greek," transformed into the act of interracial reconciliation, leads to our taking seriously the different personal
and cultural character of individuals from a minority. The
same applies to the relationship between man and woman,
to which is tied the whole problem of identity, and of
sexuality. Here the traditional Christian models, many of
which have been patriarchical and vertical, will have to
be modified by much more dynamic models. The woman
is no longer obeying the man; sexuality is being built into
the search for identity. I do not mean that the cosmic
language is responsible for the changes that take place in
the realm of sexual relationship; but I do claim that both
the relation of the sexes and personality development
have to be understood in much more dynamic terms and
that the disappearance of the pyramidal, vertical, and
stable language patterns in favor of the patterns of rhythm
and dynamism are not cause for despair, despite the crisis
they are producing between the generations, but can become a creative transformation. These new models will

help us to find new types of structures within which we can operate.

No such structures of human encounter can be a viable option unless they begin to deal with our planet as a whole. We fly across the ocean in a few hours and we share the news about a bloodbath in Malaysia on the day it occurs. We are becoming conscious as we have never been before of living in one world. But the world is not living as if it were one. The United Nations has become a frightfully frustrating experience for all who participate in it and who watch its course. What contribution is possible from my perspective? Not the romantic hope of a world family, a hope that is a long way in the future, but the courageous attempt at human encounters. We cannot let the threat of new world wars be aggravated without trying to reconcile people at all levels and occasions possible. The constant interchange of students, the meeting of political and religious groups, the travel, the exchanges of artistic and intellectual creativity, all this must become part of our programs. To be sure, the exchange will probably for the time create as little one world as the Roman imperial sphere, which gave scope to the rising Christian church, created a really unified church. But what will come out is the consciousness of a worldwide task, precisely the way the ancient church developed the awareness of a large Mediterranean catholicity despite its tensions and plurality. When I speak for the worldwide encounter I do not advocate any kind of cheap syncretism. We are not all the same, and we do not think alike. Sometimes in meetings with the East I become aware of how Western I am, just as the American theologian in the encounter with Europeans becomes aware of how American he is. But when we dare to expose ourselves beyond the first superficial contacts and attempt to understand despite all differences and frustrations we are fulfilling the common task in our human enterprise.

MATT. 8:20 AND MAN IN THE ORWELLIAN WORLD

Every age in the two-thousand-year history of the church has sought for new Christological images. Under the Vatican church, the archaeologists found Christ as Helios. In Byzantine mosaics, we see him as Pantocrator. In Romanesque art, Christ became the judge of the world. The consecutive ages have taken along some of these images, discarded others, and above all have created new ones. The newest ones betray the truth that the search for Christological images is the search for man. I want to present one aspect of the contemporary search for meaningful humanness by juxtaposing the sense of human loneliness implied in Jesus' famous words on the foxes and the birds with the image of human agony in the bronze crucifix by the French sculptress Germaine Richier.

Jesus' anguished cry, "The foxes have holes and the birds have their nests but the son of man has no place where to lay his head" (Matt. 8:20) yields one of the great eschatological insights into Jesus as man. Here is the man from Nazareth who left his family, who was driven across Galilee and Judea as much by his own demons as by the theologians of his age, who won to his side a zealous group of disciples, who was betrayed by them and finally condemned to death by the secular governor of Palestine.

In the Alpine town of Assis near Chamonix, the French artist community, inspired by some venturesome Catholic priests, created a church for the tuberculosis sanatorium there. The great artists of France, Léger, Matisse, Rouault, Chagall, Lipschitz, and many others, donated their talents to this church, which has since become one of the famous centers of modern French art. One of the most moving works in that building is the bronze sculpture of the dying Christ, which was Germaine Richier's contribution. It is a terrifying figure of tortured humanity, full of agony, distorted by horror, lonesomeness, and pain. The bishop of the diocese was so incensed by this profanation of Christ's divinity (a modern instance of secularization, perhaps) that he forbade the display of the sculpture in the choir. The conflict that evolved around this crucifix epitomizes the intensity of resistance to new visions in theology, for Germaine Richier was not only depicting a new image of Christ but was embodying in it a new image of man. Perhaps what the bishop feared most was the second, implying, as it does, what the church would condemn as secularization.

I do not intend to present an exegesis of the New Testament text and its context. Instead I want to raise the two questions that a contemporary man might ask when he faces the comparison between the human image implicit in Jesus' words and that displayed in the sculpture: With which man can I identify? What type of man do I hope to become?

When the fourth century created Christ the Pantocrator in the churches' mosaics, the believer was asked to turn toward the kingly prince, the Christian emperor in his glorious robes. Of course, there were other images of Christ at that time. So it is today, each more or less relevant according to an observer's purpose and direction. I should like to set the Christ pictures by Werner Salman and Salvador Dali alongside the crucifix by Germaine Richier in order to present the choices among which theology must come to discriminate.

In Salman's Christ, hanging on the walls of so many church narthexes and pastors' studies, the viewer identifies with the image of a comfortable middle-class Swede. He is a mild man, undisturbed, nonaggressive, benevolent, with soft locks and gentle blue eyes. The Christian who identifies with this Christ identifies with an unthreatening father image, a loving and pious yet strangely distant face that lacks the torture of the man from Nazareth who expected the Kingdom to come and whose Kingdom, after all, did not come. The crucified Christ of Dali is as

Southern European as Salman's is Northern. It is an ideal-
ized figure, a demigod somewhere between heaven and
earth, an empyreal visionary, who hangs on the cross to
be sure, but whose beautiful hands are not hurt by the
nails. It is a docetic Christ, an image of orthodoxy, above
the turmoil of daily life. Even the perspective of the
painter from above the cross emphasizes the nonearthly
character of this crucified Christ.

In some ways these two images are far apart. In the one
is the glow of Spain's vivid colors, in the other the Nordic
piety of Sweden; there Catholic orthodoxy in its visionary
docetism, here Protestant personalism with its introspec-
tion. And yet as we set them over against the crucifix
by Richier they both lack precisely what her bronze
brings out: the agony of man. The cry arising from the
tortured earth. The man who has no place to lay his head.

The crucified of Richier is lost. He is lost in the Orwellian world, in which Russian tanks overrun the Czechs
in acts of pure military brutality, in which the American
police see an enemy of the people in every student carrying a protest sign. The Orwellian world is that of the
machine to whom the individual has given over power
of decision, and that of the immense corporation on whose
payroll the individual has become a number in the com-
puter. Richier's man is crushed by that world. Like the
people in Pinter's *Birthday Party* he has no place to go,
nowhere to turn.

With which one does the Christian identify? This is
the question theology has to ask anew as it sets out to
examine its course in the future. To be sure, there are
many symbols other than this crucifix with which modern
man identifies. A whole sector of America identifies with
the beauty queen, the new symbol of the woman; another
equally large segment identifies with the centerfold nude,
symbolic of a whole revolution of sexuality and personality that is in process. A generation of young adults, for

instance, identified with the brutal masculinity of James Bond, and so forth. When I identify with Richier's man I am affirming a specific type of agony in myself and in the world, and I am expressing a protest against the conditions producing that agony.

Photography has brought that agony to our eyes time and again. We have all seen the picture of a Jewish boy, taken in the Warsaw ghetto, with a German SS soldier pointing his gun triumphantly against him. And we are haunted by the picture, appearing in many of the great journals of the world, of a Vietnamese woman staring out of stricken, emptied eyes with her dead child in her arms.

When I identify with this humanity I enter the depth of man's and of my own loneliness. I become Kafka's K. trying to find the tribunal, the judge, the sentence, and I see in my fellow human beings the four characters who wait in vain for the arrival of Godot. This identification with the tortured man in me and around me has deep theological implications. The great temptation for orthodox Christianity has been its constant slipping into docetism, despite its attempts to qualify it. The identification with the desperate figure of Richier is the strongest contemporary alternative to traditional Christological docetism. This is not an ideal figure. Instead it reminds us of the final word of Jesus in the Gospel of Mark: "My God, my God, why did you forsake me?" Theology *must* ask whether Jesus really cried as one who was forsaken. Or to put it differently: Could he have come down from the cross? When one calls on a patient in the hospital and tries to say a meaningful word to him who is dying, one knows that none has a chance to come down. Will the thought of Christology that Christ could have come down comfort a single one of them? For centuries theology thought so. I do not. And I believe we can only begin to talk credibly to the world again once we come to this position, to this identification with a person who has lost the way. I sometimes feel my own helplessness at the open sea.

From the tentativeness and precariousness of my own humanity I would say that theology has to accept the Richier image of Christ. There are those who will object that hers is not an image of Christ but an image only of man. That "only" is one of the most tragic, misleading, and defensive words in all theology. For the way to humanity is through that "only." Christ has always been called the real man, the authentic man. And it is precisely in Richier's picture, where he is most human, that he is most real: the man who has no place to lay his head. This lostness is not something to deny or to disregard. In doing so for so long, theology has imposed an unreal and dogmatic model not on Christ alone but on all human beings. It must begin to accept man as he is, in his humanness. Then it will stop offering him an illusory heaven and will be able to join him in the reshaping of the world.

What is it to be human? To cry and to touch and to laugh and to know; to venture, to lose, and to try again; to cause pain and to create; to play with the images of our minds; to surrender.

What is human? To look at the foxes and the birds and to write poetry about it. To be driven across the earth without the holes of the foxes and the nests of the birds. And to affirm, no matter how much it tears at us that it is meaningful and worthwhile to live without a resting place.

And finally, to be human is to feast and to celebrate. Ignatius of Antioch spoke about the cosmic dance in which the stars danced a chorus around the central star, the one that came down to earth. In this demonic world, we still need the dance. The ancient church in its liturgy, in its artistic joy, in its color, sensed this. Perhaps no vision can be sustained without it. It is as Walter Van Tilburg

Clark saw in his *The City of Trembling Leaves,* "The world is rolling over to expose the moon." We are aware of the incredible speed with which it is "swinging bodily through emptiness." Nevertheless, with our fingers on the edge of the pool we can cling to a flying world, feeling confusedly "the beauty and unhappiness of mortality."

Notes

CHAPTER I

INTRODUCTION—SECULARIZATION AND PROTESTANT FAITH

1. Charles Dickens, *A Tale of Two Cities* (Modern Library, Inc., 1950), p. 3.

2. David Martin, a British sociologist, has engaged in a work of "demolition" on the term "secularization." Martin suggests that the term hides rather than discloses important issues because it is so implicated in ideological perspectives. For this reason, he argues, the term should be discarded: "Secularization is less a scientific concept than a tool of counter-religious ideologies. Such ideologies select certain phenomena as *really* 'religious,' for the purposes of their own practical politics and according to the logic of their metaphysical systems." (Martin, "Towards Eliminating the Concept of Secularization," in *Penguin Survey of the Social Sciences 1965*, ed. by Julius Gould, p. 169; Penguin Books, Inc., 1965.)

That the concept of secularization has often appeared in an ideological context cannot be denied (cf. Hermann Lübbe's fine study, *Säkularisierung: Geschichte eines ideenpolitischen Begriffs;* Freiburg: Karl Alber, 1965). But the central question is whether the ideological tincture and the ambiguity of the concept of secularization require its elimination (cf. Larry Shiner's article, which appears in this volume).

3. Karl Barth, *The Epistle to the Romans* (London: Oxford University Press, 1933), p. 127. Also see *Church Dogmatics,* Vol. I, Part 2 (Edinburgh: T. & T. Clark, 1956), esp. pp. 297–325.

4. Dietrich Bonhoeffer, *Prisoner for God: Letters and Papers from Prison,* ed. by Eberhard Bethge (The Macmillan Company, 1954), pp. 126, 148.

5. *Ibid.,* p. 168.

6. *Ibid.,* p. 122.

7. Arend van Leeuwen, *Christianity in World History* (London: Edinburgh House Press, 1964), p. 409.

8. See especially Friedrich Gogarten, *The Reality of Faith*, tr. by Carl Michalson, *et al.* (The Westminster Press, 1959), and *Verhängnis und Hoffnung der Neuzeit: Die Säkularisierung als theologishes Problem* (Stuttgart: Friedrich Vorkwerk, 1953). Also see Larry Shiner, *The Secularization of History* (Abingdon Press, 1966).

9. Jacques Ellul, *The Technological Society* (Vintage Books, Random House, Inc., 1967), p. 36.

Not all arguments for a causal relation between certain religious symbols and institutions and secularization are as ridiculous as Ellul suggests. Offering an alternative to the Marxian interpretation of religion and society, Max Weber examined the possible causal relation between Protestantism and some salient features of the modern world in his seminal work, *The Protestant Ethic and the Spirit of Capitalism* (Charles Scribner's Sons, 1958). He argued that the symbol system of Calvinism was a significant factor in the emergence of the "spirit" of rational bourgeois capitalism, but he did not attempt to replace Marxian reductionism with a simplistic causal scheme. Ernst Troeltsch also focused on the impact of Protestantism on the rise of the modern world (see *Protestantism and Progress;* Beacon Press, Inc., 1958). For him Protestantism had "totalistic impulses" (Eisenstadt's term), just as medieval religion, but it did contribute *indirectly* to the emergence of the modern world in that it helped undermine some of the existing barriers: "While Protestantism has furthered the rise of the modern world, often largely and decisively, in none of these departments [family, law, state, economics, society, science, and art] does it appear as its actual creator. What it has done is simply to secure for it greater freedom of development." (P. 171.)

More recently, Peter Berger has contended that there is a relationship of historical causality (in contrast to logical realization) between Christianity and secularization. Berger writes: "The question, 'Why in the modern West?' asked with respect to the phenomenon of secularization, must be answered at least in part by looking at its roots in the religious tradition of the modern West." (*The Sacred Canopy*, pp. 124–125; Doubleday & Company, Inc., 1967.) For a more Marxian interpretation, one can examine Alasdair MacIntyre's *Seculariza-*

tion and Moral Change (Oxford University Press, Inc., 1967), which emphasizes almost exclusively material factors such as industrialization and urbanization.

Much recent discussion of religion and social change, including secularization, has focused on the developing nations. Its major topic has been religion and modernization. Examples of this literature, and the arguments that have emerged, are Robert Bellah (ed.), *Religion and Progress in Modern Asia* (The Free Press, 1965), and S. N. Eisenstadt (ed.), *The Protestant Ethic and Modernization: A Comparative View* (Basic Books, Inc., Publishers, 1968). The significant issues in these various debates should not be obscured by Ellul's blanket repudiation.

10. Van Leeuwen, *op. cit.*, p. 331.

11. Ellul, *op. cit.*, pp. 428–429.

12. Julian N. Hartt, "Modern Images of Man." Unpublished.

13. See Franklin L. Baumer, *Religion and the Rise of Scepticism* (Harcourt, Brace, and World, Inc., 1960), pp. 237–240.

14. Robert Nisbet, "The Impact of Technology on Ethical Decision-Making," in *Religion and Social Conflict,* ed. by Robert Lee and Martin E. Marty (Oxford University Press, Inc., 1964), pp. 10–11.

15. For an excellent analysis of these trends, see Thomas W. Ogletree, "From Anxiety to Responsibility: The Shifting Focus of Theological Reflection," in *New Theology No. 6,* ed. by Martin Marty and Dean Peerman (The Macmillan Company, 1969), pp. 35–65.

16. One example of a functional justification of religion is Richard Rubenstein's interpretation of Judaism. Cf. *After Auschwitz: Radical Theology and Contemporary Judaism* (The Bobbs-Merrill Company, Inc., 1965).

17. See, *inter alia,* Lionel S. Thornton, *Revelation and the Modern World* (London: The Dacre Press, 1950).

18. Cf. Paul Lehmann's koinonia ethics as delineated in *Ethics in a Christian Context* (Harper & Row, Publishers, Inc., 1963).

19. See David Baily Harned, *The Ambiguity of Religion* (The Westminster Press, 1968).

20. Langdon Gilkey, "Unbelief and the Secular Spirit," in Christopher F. Mooney (ed.), *The Presence and Absence of God* (Fordham University Press, 1969), p. 52.

21. Robert Bellah, "The Sociology of Religion," in *American Sociology*, ed. by Talcott Parsons (Basic Books, Inc., Publishers, 1968), p. 222.

22. Berger, *op. cit.*, p. 182. Actually he is interested in showing the threat of sociology to the theologian on the *existential* rather than the *methodological* level.

23. For a criticism of Luckmann's definition of religion, see Berger, *op. cit.*, Appendix I, "Sociological Definitions of Religion."

24. Little work has been done on these questions from a theological standpoint; the best studies to date focus on the social sciences in relation to ethics and policy-making. See, for example, Gibson Winter, *Elements for a Social Ethic* (The Macmillan Company, 1966), and Max F. Millikan, "Inquiry and Policy: The Relation of Knowledge to Action," in *The Human Meaning of the Social Sciences*, ed. by Daniel Lerner (Meridian Books, The World Publishing Company, 1963), pp. 158–180.

CHAPTER II

THE MEANINGS OF SECULARIZATION, *by Larry Shiner*

1. J. M. Yinger, *Religion, Society and the Individual* (The Macmillan Company, 1957), p. 119.

2. R. S. Lynd and H. M. Lynd, *Middletown* (Harcourt, Brace and World, Inc., 1929), p. 112.

3. J. T. Flint, "The Secularization of Norwegian Society," in *Comparative Studies in Society and History*, Vol. VI (1964), pp. 325–344.

4. P. A. Sorokin, "The Western Religion and Morality of Today," in *International Yearbook for the Sociology of Religion*, Vol. II (Köln und Opladen, 1966), pp. 10, 13.

5. *Ibid.*, pp. 19–20.

6. D. A. Martin, "Utopian Aspects of the Concept of Secularization," in *International Yearbook for the Sociology of Religion*, Vol. II (Köln und Opladen, 1966), p. 92.

7. G. Le Bras, "Dechristianisation: mot fallacieux," in *Social Compass*, Vol. X (1963), pp. 448, 451.

8. H. Pfautz, "Christian Science: A Case Study of the Social Psychological Aspect of Secularization," in *Social Forces*, Vol. 34 (1956), p. 246.

9. A. von Harnack, *Monasticism: Its Ideals and History* (London, 1901), p. 112.

10. H. Pfautz, "The Sociology of Secularization: Religious Groups," in *American Journal of Sociology*, Vol. 61 (1955), pp. 121–128.

11. T. Parsons, "Christianity and Modern Industrial Society," in *Sociological Theory, Values, and Sociocultural Change*, ed. by E. A. Tiryakian (The Free Press of Glencoe, Inc., 1963), pp. 33–70. See excerpt from the article, in this volume.

12. E. Kahler, *Man the Measure* (Pantheon Books, Inc., 1943), p. 333.

13. Cf. "Science as a Vocation," in *From Max Weber, Essays in Sociology*, ed. and tr. by H. H. Gerth and C. W. Mills (Oxford University Press, Inc., 1946), p. 139.

14. M. Eliade, *The Sacred and the Profane* (A Harper Torchbook, 1961), p. 17.

15. R. Mehl, "De la sécularisation à l'atheism," in *Foi et Vie*, Vol. 65 (1966), p. 70.

16. B. Grotheuysen, "Secularism," in *Encyclopædia of the Social Sciences*, Vol. XIII (1934), p. 634.

17. D. von Oppen, "Die Säkularisation als soziologisches Problem," in *Evangelisch-Lutherische Kirchenzeitung*, Vol. XII, No. 23 (Dec. 1, 1958), p. 380.

18. Grotheuysen, *loc. cit.*, p. 631.

19. T. Rendtorff, "Zur Säkularisierungsproblematik," in *International Yearbook for the Sociology of Religion*, Vol. II (Köln und Opladen, 1966), p. 54.

20. E. Troeltsch, *Protestantism and Progress* (Beacon Press, Inc., 1958) p. 96.

21. E. Troeltsch, *Der Historismus und seine Probleme* (Tübingen, 1922), p. 57.

22. Cf. R. Wittram, "Möglichkeiten und Grenzen der Geschichtswissenschaft in der Gegenwart," in *Zeitschrift für Theologie und Kirche*, Vol. 62 (1965), pp. 430–457. H. Desroche, *Marxisme et Religions* (Paris, 1962).

23. C. Y. Glock and R. Stark, *Religion and Society in Tension* (Rand McNally & Company, 1965), pp. 2–8.

24. N. Berkes, "Religious and Secular Institutions in Comparative Perspective," in *Archives de Sociologie des Religions,* Vol. 8 (1963), pp. 65–72.

25. Rendtorff, *op. cit.,* p. 61.

CHAPTER III

CHRISTIANITY AND MODERN INDUSTRIAL SOCIETY, *by Talcott Parsons*

1. *Sociological Theory, Values, and Sociocultural Change,* ed. by Edward A. Tiryakian (The Free Press of Glencoe, Inc., 1963).

2. T. Parsons, "Christianity and Modern Industrial Society," in *Sociological Theory and Modern Society* (The Free Press of Glencoe, Inc., 1967), p. 388.

3. *Ibid.,* p. 396.

4. By "autonomy" I mean here *independence* of direct authoritarian control combined with *responsibility* defined in moral-religious terms. It is close to "theonomy" as that concept is used by Tillich.

5. This thesis is further developed in my two essays published as Ch. III and IV of *Structure and Process in Modern Societies* (The Free Press of Glencoe, Inc., 1960).

6. Basing myself on the studies of voting behavior by Berelson, Lazarsfeld, *et al.,* I have analyzed this situation in " 'Voting' and the Equilibrium of the American Political System," *American Voting Behavior,* ed. by Eugene Burdick and Arthur J. Brodbeck (The Free Press of Glencoe, Inc., 1959).

7. Cf. T. Parsons and W. White, "The Link between Character and Society," in *Culture and Social Character,* ed. by S. M. Lipset and L. Loewenthal (The Free Press of Glencoe, Inc., 1961), reprinted in my *Social Structure and Personality* (The Free Press of Glencoe, Inc., 1964).

CHAPTER IV

THE INVISIBLE RELIGION, *by Thomas Luckmann*

1. A large body of literature was devoted to the study of and theories about this process. There is little doubt that the

most incisive and seminal discussion of this process is that of Max Weber.

2. The analysis of the general social-psychological implications and consequences of institutional segmentation is based, in the main points, on Arnold Gehlen, *Die Seele im technischen Zeitalter: Sozialpsychologische Probleme der industriellen Gesellschaft* (Tübingen: Mohr [Siebeck], 1949). Reference should also be made to a recent typology of social orders that takes into account, among other things, the degree of institutional specialization in the social structure and articulates its consequences for socialization processes. Cf. Friedrich Tenbruck, *Geschichte und Gesellschaft* (unpublished *Habilitationsschrift*, University of Freiburg, 1962).

3. Cf. Peter Berger and Thomas Luckmann, "Secularization and Pluralism," in *International Yearbook for the Sociology of Religion*, Vol. II (1966).

4. Cf. Helmut Schelsky, "Ist die Dauerreflektion institutionalisierbar?" in *Zeitschrift für evangelische Ethik*, 1:4, pp. 153–174.

5. Cf., for example, W. Pickering, "Quelques résultats d'interviews religieuses," in E. Collard and others (eds.), *Vocation de la sociologie religieuse; sociologie des vocations* (Tournai: Casterman, 1958), pp. 54–76. Also, J. J. Dumont, "Sondage sur la mentalité religieuse d'ouvriers en Wallonie," *ibid.*, pp. 77–113. Also, Hans Otto Woelber, *Religion ohne Entscheidung: Volkskirche am Beispiel der jungen Generation* (Göttingen: Vandenhoeck & Ruprecht, 1959). Also Thomas Luckmann, "Four Protestant Parishes in Germany," in *Social Research*, 26:4 (1959), pp. 443–446. Cf. also, Louis Schneider and Sanford M. Dornbusch, *Popular Religion—Inspirational Books in America* (The University of Chicago Press, 1958).

6. Cf. Friedrich Tenbruck, "Die Kirchengemeinde in der entkirchlichten Gesellschaft," in *Soziologie der Kirchengemeinde*, ed. by Dietrich Goldschmidt, *et al.* (Stuttgart: Enke, 1959).

7. Cf., for example, The Report of the President's Commission on National Goals, *Goals for Americans* (Prentice-Hall, Inc., 1950). Cf. also the analysis of the post-Korea "Militant Liberty" Programs of the U.S. Department of Defense, in Morris Janowitz, *The Professional Soldier* (The Free Press of Glencoe, Inc., 1960).

8. Cf. Peter Berger and Thomas Luckmann, "Sociology of Religion and Sociology of Knowledge," in *Sociology and Social Research*, 47:4 (1963).

9. Cf. Tenbruck, "Die Kirchengemeinde in der entkirchlichten Gesellschaft," *loc. cit.*

10. Cf. Peter Berger and Hansfried Kellner, "Marriage and the Construction of Reality," *Diogène*, 46:2 (1964), pp. 3–32.

11. Cf. Hansfried Kellner, *Dimensions of the Individual's Conception of Social Reality Arising Within Marriage* (unpublished Ph.D. dissertation, Graduate Faculty, The New School for Social Research, 1966).

12. David Riesman's analysis of "other-direction" is highly pertinent here. He provides a general perspective in which the importance of "significant others" in providing support for the individual can be understood as a consequence of the fact that clear-cut socialization profiles are not available in a relatively mobile urban-industrial society. Cf. David Riesman with Nathan Glazer and Reuel Denney, *The Lonely Crowd* (Yale University Press, 1950).

13. Cf. Thomas J. W. Wilson with Everett Meyers, *Wife Swapping: A Complete Eight Year Survey of Morals in America* (New York, 1965).

14. Cf. Peter Berger, "Towards a Sociological Understanding of Psychoanalysis," in *Social Research*, 32:1 (1965), pp. 26–41.

15. For the classical discussion of the mobility ethos and its social-psychological impressions, cf. Robert Merton, *Social Theory and Social Structure* (The Free Press of Glencoe, Inc., 1957; rev. ed.), pp. 131–194.

16. Thomas Luckmann and Peter Berger, "Social Mobility and Personal Identity," in *European Journal of Sociology*, 5:2 (1964), pp. 331–344.

CHAPTER V

CIVIL RELIGION IN AMERICA, *by Robert N. Bellah*

1. Why something so obvious should have escaped serious analytical attention is in itself an interesting problem. Part of the reason is probably the controversial nature of the subject. From the earliest years of the nineteenth century, conservative

religious and political groups have argued that Christianity is, in fact, the national religion. Some of them have from time to time and as recently as the 1950's proposed constitutional amendments that would explicitly recognize the sovereignty of Christ. In defending the doctrine of separation of church and state, opponents of such groups have denied that the national polity has, intrinsically, anything to do with religion at all. The moderates on this issue have insisted that the American state has taken a permissive and indeed supportive attitude toward religious groups (tax exemption, etc.), thus favoring religion but still missing the positive institutionalization with which I am concerned. But part of the reason this issue has been left in obscurity is certainly due to the peculiarly Western concept of "religion" as denoting a single type of collectivity of which an individual can be a member of one and only one at a time. The Durkheimian notion that every group has a religious dimension, which would be seen as obvious in southern or eastern Asia, is foreign to us. This obscures the recognition of such dimensions in our society.

2. Quoted in Will Herberg, *Protestant—Catholic—Jew* (Doubleday & Company, Inc., 1955), p. 97.

3. God is mentioned or referred to in all inaugural addresses but Washington's second, which is a very brief (two paragraphs) and perfunctory acknowledgment. It is not without interest that the actual word *God* does not appear until Monroe's second inaugural, 5 March 1821. In his first inaugural, Washington refers to God as "that Almighty Being who rules the universe," "Great Author of every public and private good," "Invisible Hand," and "benign Parent of the Human Race." John Adams refers to God as "Providence," "Being who is supreme over all," "Patron of Order," "Fountain of Justice," and "Protector in all ages of the world of virtuous liberty." Jefferson speaks of "that Infinite Power which rules the destinies of the universe," and "that Being in whose hands we are." Madison speaks of "that Almighty Being whose power regulates the destiny of nations," and "Heaven." Monroe uses "Providence" and "the Almighty" in his first inaugural and finally "Almighty God" in his second. See *Inaugural Addresses of the Presidents of the United States from George Washington 1789 to Harry S. Truman 1949,* 82d Congress, 2d Session, House Document No. 540, 1952.

4. For example, Abiel Abbot, pastor of the First Church in Haverhill, Massachusetts, delivered a Thanksgiving sermon in 1799, *Traits of Resemblance in the People of the United States of America to Ancient Israel,* in which he said: "It has been often remarked that the people of the United States come nearer to a parallel with Ancient Israel, than any other nation upon the globe. Hence OUR AMERICAN ISRAEL is a term frequently used; and common consent allows it apt and proper." Cited in Hans Kohn, *The Idea of Nationalism* (The Macmillan Company, 1961), p. 665.

5. That the Mosaic analogy was present in the minds of leaders at the very moment of the birth of the republic is indicated in the designs proposed by Franklin and Jefferson for a seal of the United States of America. Together with Adams, they formed a committee of three delegated by the Continental Congress on July 4, 1776, to draw up the new device. "Franklin proposed as the device Moses lifting up his wand and dividing the Red Sea while Pharaoh was overwhelmed by its waters, with the motto 'Rebellion to tyrants is obedience to God.' Jefferson proposed the children of Israel in the wilderness 'led by a cloud by day and a pillar of fire at night.'" Anson Phelps Stokes, *Church and State in the United States,* Vol. 1 (Harper & Brothers, 1950), pp. 467–468.

6. Sidney Mead, *The Lively Experiment* (Harper & Row, Publishers, Inc., 1963), p. 12.

7. Quoted by Arthur Lehman Goodhart in Allan Nevins (ed.), *Lincoln and the Gettysburg Address* (University of Illinois Press, 1964), p. 39.

8. *Ibid.,* "On the Gettysburg Address," pp. 88–89.

9. Quoted in G. Sherwood Eddy, *The Kingdom of God and the American Dream* (Harper & Brothers, 1941), p. 162.

10. Karl Decker and Angus McSween, *Historic Arlington* (Washington, D.C., 1892), pp. 60–67.

11. How extensive the activity associated with Memorial Day can be is indicated by Warner: "The sacred symbolic behavior of Memorial Day, in which scores of the town's organizations are involved, is ordinarily divided into four periods. During the year separate rituals are held by many of the associations for their dead, and many of these activities are connected with later Memorial Day events. In the second phase, preparations are made during the last three or four

weeks for the ceremony itself, and some of the associations perform public rituals. The third phase consists of scores of rituals held in all the cemeteries, churches, and halls of the associations. These rituals consist of speeches and highly ritualized behavior. They last for two days and are climaxed by the fourth and last phase, in which all the separate celebrants gather in the center of the business district on the afternoon of Memorial Day. The separate organizations, with their members in uniform or with fitting insignia, march through the town, visit the shrines and monuments of the hero dead, and, finally, enter the cemetery. Here dozens of ceremonies are held, most of them highly symbolic and formalized." During these various ceremonies Lincoln is continually referred to and the Gettysburg Address recited many times. W. Lloyd Warner, *American Life* (The University of Chicago Press, 1962), pp. 8–9.

12. Reinhold Niebuhr, "The Religion of Abraham Lincoln," in Nevins (ed.), *op. cit.*, p. 72. William J. Wolf of the Episcopal Theological School in Cambridge, Massachusetts, has written: "Lincoln is one of the greatest theologians of America— not in the technical meaning of producing a system of doctrine, certainly not as the defender of some one denomination, but in the sense of seeing the hand of God intimately in the affairs of nations. Just so the prophets of Israel criticized the events of their day from the perspective of the God who is concerned for history and who reveals His will within it. Lincoln now stands among God's latter-day prophets." (*The Religion of Abraham Lincoln*, p. 24; The Seabury Press, Inc., 1963.)

13. Seymour Martin Lipset, *The First New Nation* (William Heinemann, Ltd., 1964), Ch. 4, "Religion and American Values."

14. Alexis de Tocqueville, *Democracy in America*, Vol. 1 (Vintage Books, Random House, Inc., 1954), p. 310.

15. Henry Bargy, *La Religion dans la Societé aux États-Unis* (Paris, 1902), p. 31.

16. De Tocqueville, *op. cit.*, p. 311. Later he says: "In the United States even the religion of most of the citizens is republican, since it submits the truths of the other world to private judgment, as in politics the care of their temporal interests is abandoned to the good sense of the people. Thus

every man is allowed freely to take that road which he thinks will lead him to heaven, just as the law permits every citizen to have the right of choosing his own government." (P. 436.)

17. U.S. *Congressional Record*, House, 15 March 1965, pp. 4924, 4926.

18. See Louis Hartz, "The Feudal Dream of the South," Part 4, *The Liberal Tradition in America* (Harcourt, Brace and World, Inc., 1955).

19. Speech of Senator J. William Fulbright of 28 April 1966, as reported in *The New York Times*, 29 April 1966.

20. Quoted in Yehoshua Arieli, *Individualism and Nationalism in American Ideology* (Harvard University Press, 1964), p. 274.

CHAPTER VI

COMMUNITY—CHRISTIAN AND SECULAR, *by Charles C. West*

1. This definition was first offered as a tentative working proposition in a background paper for a consultation on "The Meaning of the Secular" for university teachers at the Ecumenical Institute, Bossey, Sept., 1959. It was again reflected in the report of this consultation, which is available from the Ecumenical Institute (Château de Bossey, Céligny, Switzerland). The discussion on the subject was continued in a European conference of the World's Student Christian Federation in Graz, Austria, in 1962, and in its staff meeting in Jan., 1963. The papers from these meetings are published in *The Student World* (13, rue Calvin, Geneva, Switzerland), No. 1, 1963. See especially Steven Mackie, "European Christians and the Secular Debate," pp. 4 ff.

2. Guardini, *Das Ende der Neuzeit* (The End of Our Time), tr. by Buras and Oates (Würzburg: Werkbund Verlag, 1950), p. 77.

3. Summary of Professor Mehl's remarks in the report of the conference of the Ecumenical Institute on "The Meaning of the Secular," *op. cit.*, Appendix, p. 7. See also "La Sécularisation de la cité," in *Le Problème de la civilisation chrétienne* (Presses Universitaires de France, 1958).

4. Carl J. Friedrich, *Transcendent Justice* (Duke University Press, 1964), p. 116.

5. Cornelis van Peursen, "Man and Reality—The History of Human Thought," in *The Student World*, No. 1 (1963), pp. 13 f.

6. Arend van Leeuwen, *Christianity in World History* (London: Edinburgh House Press, 1964), Ch. IV.

7. See, for example, Martin Buber, *The Prophetic Faith*; J. Pedersen, *Israel*; G. Ernest Wright, *The Old Testament Against Its Environment, et al.* A good summary of the argument is found in Van Leeuwen, *op. cit.*, Chs. II, III.

8. I am grateful to Ian Ramsey for the reminder that such a metaphysical task is possible. Cf. also S. N. Hampshire, "Metaphysical Systems," in *The Nature of Metaphysics*, ed. by D. F. Pears (London: The Macmillan Company, 1958).

9. Karl Barth, *Kirchliche Dogmatik*, II/i, p. 203.

10. H. R. Niebuhr, *The Responsible Self* (Harper & Row, Publishers, Inc., 1963), p. 164.

11. *Ibid.*, p. 138.

12. Barth, *op. cit.*, III/2, p. 64.

CHAPTER VII

RELIGION, MORALITY, AND SECULARIZATION,
by David Little

1. See particularly Max Weber, *Religion of China* (The Free Press of Glencoe, Inc., 1964); *Religion of India* (The Free Press of Glencoe, Inc., 1958); and *The Sociology of Religion* (Beacon Press, Inc., 1963).

2. P. H. Nowell-Smith, "Morality: Religious and Secular," in *Christian Ethics and Contemporary Philosophy*, ed. by Ian T. Ramsey (The Macmillan Company, 1966), p. 95.

3. *Ibid.*, p. 104.

4. Rodney Stark and Charles Y. Glock, "Will Ethics Be the Death of Christianity?" in *Transaction*, Vol. V, No. 7 (June, 1968).

5. *Ibid.*, p. 12.

6. Talcott Parsons, "Christianity and Modern Industrial Society," in *Sociological Theory, Values, and Sociocultural Change*, ed. by E. A. Tiryakian (The Free Press of Glencoe, Inc., 1963). See excerpt from the article, in this volume.

7. Ernest Barker, "Roman Conception of Empire," in

Church, State and Education (University of Michigan Press, 1957), p. 20.

8. *Ancient Roman Religion*, ed. by F. C. Grant (Liberal Arts Press, Inc., 1957), p. 174.

9. Rudolf Bultmann, *Primitive Christianity in Its Contemporary Setting* (Meridian Books, The World Publishing Company, 1956), p. 158.

10. Joseph Klausner, *Jesus of Nazareth* (New York, 1925), p. 390.

11. C. N. Cochrane, *Christianity and Classical Culture* (Oxford University Press, Inc., 1957), p. 228.

12. Quoted by Cochrane, *ibid.*, p. 228.

13. Bultmann, *Theology of the New Testament* (2 vols., Charles Scribner's Sons, 1955), Vol. II, p. 98.

14. Eduard Schweizer, *Church Order in the New Testament* (London: SCM Press, Ltd., 1961), p. 100.

15. See Rudolf Schnackenburg, *The Moral Teaching of the New Testament* (Herder & Herder, Inc., 1967), pp. 151–160; and V. P. Furnish, *Theology and Ethics in Paul* (Abingdon Press, 1968), p. 80.

16. That is, the moral premise in the argument—that men ought to repay kindness with gratitude—is not substantiated, but simply assumed to be true by Paul. Though I cannot deal here with the matter, I think this shows that Paul assumes "moral reason" in much of his writings.

17. Immanuel Kant, *The Doctrine of Virtue*, tr. by M. J. Gregor (Harper & Row, Publishers, Inc., 1964), p. 123.

18. In *Religion, Order and Law* (Harper & Row, Publishers, Inc., 1969), I have analyzed these matters in detail.

19. I have in mind, for example, Michael Walzer, *The Revolution of the Saints* (Harvard University Press, 1965).

20. William Perkins, *Works* (3 vols., London, 1612–1631), Vol. II, p. 276.

Date Due